Corporate Acquisitions and Mergers in Austria

Corporate Acquisitions and Mergers in Austria

Clemens Hasenauer

Albert Birkner

CERHA HEMPEL Rechtsanwälte GmbH

This book was originally published as a chapter in Corporate Acquisitions and Mergers.

General Editor: Peter Begg

Wolters Kluwer

Published by:
Kluwer Law International B.V.
PO Box 316
2400 AH Alphen aan den Rijn
The Netherlands
E-mail: lrs-sales@wolterskluwer.com
Website: www.wolterskluwer.com/en/solutions/kluwerlawinternational

Sold and distributed by:
Wolters Kluwer Legal & Regulatory U.S.
7201 McKinney Circle
Frederick, MD 21704
United States of America
E-mail: customer.service@wolterskluwer.com

ISBN 978-94-035-2396-5

e-Book: ISBN 978-94-035-2736-9
web-PDF: ISBN 978-94-035-2746-8

Contents

CERHA HEMPEL RECHTSANWÄLTE GMBH

CERHA HEMPEL is one of the leading corporate law firms in Central and Eastern Europe with its headquarters in Vienna. With over 200 lawyers, we offer our clients superior experience and expertise in all areas of corporate and commercial law, both in Austria and in Central and Eastern Europe.

On the one hand, this requires extensive specialist knowledge, motivation and commitment, and on the other, an excellent understanding of our clients' businesses. Our organizational structure combines the resources of our core teams with specialists, enabling us to advise clients and manage transactions in the best and most efficient way possible.

At CERHA HEMPEL, we look back on a long and successful company history. Over the past twenty-five years, CERHA HEMPEL has played a key role in many of the most significant transactions in Austria. This is what really distinguishes us as one of the leading law firms in the fields of mergers and acquisitions, capital markets, banking and finance, real estate and construction, and litigation and arbitration.

CERHA HEMPEL has won numerous awards, in 2019 it was named 'Austrian Law Firm of the Year' by JUVE, in 2020 it was named 'Austria M&A Legal Adviser of the Year' by Mergermarket and in 2021 it was named 'Austria Corporate Firm of the Year' by IFLR.

Authors

Dr Clemens Hasenauer, LLM/MBA is admitted as an attorney at law in both Austria and New York and as a solicitor in England and Wales. He is managing partner at CERHA HEMPEL, where he specializes in large cross-border transactions.

Dr Albert Birkner, LLM (Cantab.) is admitted as an attorney at law in both Austria and the Czech Republic. He is managing partner at CERHA HEMPEL and specializes in M&A, takeovers, private equity and private trusts.

1 INTRODUCTION

[01] Located in Southern Central Europe, with a land surface area of 83,878.99 square kilometres and a population of almost 9 m, the Republic of Austria extends from the Alps to the Danube Region, sharing common borders with Germany, the Czech Republic, Slovakia, Hungary, Slovenia, Italy, Switzerland and Liechtenstein. It has been a member country of the European Union (EU) since the mid-1990s and is known for its highly sophisticated and reliable legal and judicial system, its highly qualified and skilled labour workforce and its friendly and stable investment climate. Due to its geographical location in the heart of Europe and its long historical, political and cultural ties with the neighbouring countries in Eastern Europe, Austria is the ideal hub to the Central and Eastern European Region, often used as bridge and starting point for doing business in Eastern and Southeastern Europe.

2 LOCAL ECONOMIC, POLITICAL AND CULTURAL ASPECTS

2.1 Country Profile

[02] Austria is a federal state consisting of nine provinces (*Bundesländer*): Burgenland, Carinthia (*Kärnten*), Lower Austria (*Niederösterreich*), Salzburg, Styria (*Steiermark*), Tyrol (*Tirol*), Upper Austria (*Oberösterreich*), Vienna (*Wien*) and Vorarlberg. Austria's capital, and also its largest city, is Vienna.

[03] As of 1 January 2022, Austria had a population of approximately 8.9 m, 1.9 m of whom live in Vienna.

[04] The official language in Austria is German, which is spoken by 98% of the citizens. However, English is also widely spoken in business, legal, touristic, academic and other professional circles. Many people in the southern parts of the country also speak Italian.

[05] On 1 January 2002, the 'Schilling' (ATS), Austria's former currency, was replaced by the common European currency 'euro' (EUR). The exchange rate was fixed by Council Regulation (EC) No. 2866/98 of 31 December 1998 on the conversion rates with the currencies of the Member States with a ratio of EUR1 = ATS13.7603.

[06] Natural resources to be found in Austria include iron ore, brown coal, crude oil and natural gas, magnesite, quartz sand, gypsum, lead and zinc ores, as well as graphite and kaolin.

[07] Austria's infrastructure is very well developed. Nearly all major cities (Graz, Innsbruck, Klagenfurt, Salzburg, Linz and Vienna) have larger airports, which are destinations for most international airlines. Public transport generally reaches high standards; the state provides a sophisticated railroad system as well as bus and tram services. In Vienna a well-developed underground system makes it easy to travel around the city.

[08] Austria has a highly skilled and well-educated workforce, which makes the country interesting for entrepreneurial as well as financial investors. Compared to the EU, labour costs are at an average level, whereas the workforce is at a higher than average skill level. As a positive result of Austria's social partnership system, labour conflicts (such as strikes) occur very rarely.

2.2 Political System

[09] According to its Constitution as of 1920, Austria is a democratic republic and a federal state. Both the Federal President and the legislative bodies are democratically elected by direct vote. The Austrian Parliament is the legislative power and consists of two chambers, the 'Nationalrat' and the 'Bundesrat'. The legislative power of the federal states is exercised by their provincial parliaments. The Austrian 'Nationalrat', which constitutes the most important governmental body of the Austrian legislative hierarchy, consists of 183 Members of Parliament, who are elected by the people every five years and who represent the interests of the whole country. The members of the 'Bundesrat' – currently 61 (the number depends on the number of citizens in each province) – are nominated by the provincial parliaments and represent the interests of the federal provinces.

[10] The supreme federal executive bodies are the Federal President (*Bundespräsident*) and the members of the Federal Government (*Bundesregierung*), headed by the Federal Chancellor (*Bundeskanzler*). The supreme state executive bodies are the Provincial Governments, each headed by the Provincial Governor (*Landeshauptmann*).

[11] Since 1 January 1995, Austria has been a member of the EU. Besides that, Austria is also a member of the most important international organizations, especially the United Nations (UN), the World Trade Organization (WTO), the Organisation for Economic Co-operation and Development (OECD) and the Organization for Security and Co-operation in Europe (OSCE).

2.3 Legal System

[12] Apart from EU law, the Austrian Federal Constitutional Law represents the top level in the tiered structure of the national legal systems. This tiered structure consists of the constitution, laws, ordinances, verdicts, and rulings. The increasing internationalization of law, and, in particular, Austria's membership of the EU, led to an extension of the traditional structure to include the supranational Community law. Austria is also a member of the European Convention on Human Rights and has even made this convention part of its constitution. The accession to the European Court of Human Rights in Strasbourg has had a lasting influence on the Austrian system of jurisdiction.

[13] The Legal Information System of the Republic of Austria makes all the general norms of federal law and state law, as well as the specific norms derived from decisions of the Constitutional Court and the Administrative Court, available to the public free of charge via internet (http://www.ris.bka.gv.at).

2.4 Economy

2.4.1 Current and Projected Growth Rates

[14] The gross domestic product of the developed market economy in Austria amounted to approximately EUR402.71 bn in 2021. It is predicted that the gross domestic product will amount to approximately EUR441 44 bn in 2022, which constitutes an increase of 9.6%.

[15] Being a member of one of the world's largest economic areas, the EU, as well as the EURO project, Austria's position in the world economy is even more strengthened.

2.4.2 M&A Trends

[16] In 2021, there were 293 M&A transactions involving Austrian companies. The transaction volume amounted to EUR9.16 bn in 2021. Three M&A transactions involving Austrian companies exceeded the volume of EUR1 bn in 2021. 133 of the 293 M&A transactions in 2021 were inbound M&A transactions, where foreign investors sought to acquire Austrian targets or their shares. The top five transactions in 2021 represented a volume of EUR6.43 bn and accounted for around 70% of Austria's total transaction volume.

[17] Strategic investors are involved in the vast majority of transactions in the Austrian M&A market. In 2021, 276 out of the 293 transactions involved strategic investors. However, there was a slight increase in transactions that involved financial investors, such as private equity or venture capital firms, from 15 in 2020 to 17 in 2021.

[18] With a total of 77 deals in 2021, the real estate sector proved to be the most attractive industry in terms of the reported number of M&A transactions in Austria, followed by companies in the industrial sector with 64 transactions and the technology sector with 59 transactions. In terms of published transaction volumes, the commercial and consumer goods sector ranks first with EUR2.4 bn, ahead of the real estate sector with EUR2.2 bn.

2.5 Cultural Aspects

2.5.1 Investment Climate

[19] The investment climate in Austria, in general, is quite favourable. Only very few restrictions exist with regard to foreign investments in Austria, mainly relating to sensitive industries and specifically regulated areas (*see* 3.4.1 and 3.4.2).

[20] Since Austria is a highly developed and politically stable country in the heart of the EU with a high level of legal security, conducting business in Austria is not considered to be risky. Furthermore, Austrian court proceedings are also very high-standard and since Austria is a member of the New York Arbitration Convention, Austrian arbitral awards are enforceable in all states that are party to such Convention.

2.5.2 Local Practices

[21] Austria has always had high standards for preventing corruption and bribery which have been further increased by European law since Austria joined the EU. The giving and acceptance of gifts is not a normal feature of business transactions, but may rather constitute a criminal offence under certain circumstances (*see* 3.7.1).

[22] There are no established local business practices or cultural issues which might represent a hurdle in the course of an M&A transaction.

3 REGULATORY FRAMEWORK

3.1 Business Vehicles

3.1.1 Overview

[23] The Austrian legal system offers, alongside the sole proprietorship, a wide variety of business entities from which to conduct business in Austria: companies (stock corporations and limited liability companies), partnerships (limited and unlimited), joint ventures or branch offices of foreign companies. The choice of entity should be carefully considered, particularly in the light of the method of governance, liability issues and tax issues.

[24] The companies' legislation is contained in various federal statutes, the most important of which are:

- Commercial Code (*Unternehmensgesetzbuch*; *UGB*).
- Limited Liability Companies Act (*Gesetz über die Gesellschaften mit beschränkter Haftung*; *GmbHG*).
- Stock Corporations Act (Aktiengesetz; AktG).

[25] The most common form of business entity is the company: the two main types of companies are the Limited Liability Company (*Gesellschaft mit beschränkter Haftung*; *GmbH*) and the Stock Corporation (*Aktiengesellschaft*; *AG*). Both companies come into legal existence upon registration with the Austrian Commercial Register (*Firmenbuch*). All documents submitted to the Commercial Register have to be in German. Documents in other languages have to be translated and legalized.

3.1.2 The Limited Liability Company (*Gesellschaft mit beschränkter Haftung; GmbH*)

[26] The limited liability company is probably the most commonly used business form in Austria. The main source of law is the Limited Liability Companies Act. The constitutional documents for the limited liability company are the Articles of Association (*Gesellschaftsvertrag*) which have to be set up in the form of a notarial deed. The Articles of Association are filed with the commercial register upon registration of the company. The registration procedure takes approximately two or three weeks.

[27] The minimum share capital of a limited liability company is EUR35 000 and may be paid up either in cash or in kind. It is also possible to start with a share capital of only EUR10 000 (*Gründungsprivilegierung*); however, there is an obligation to raise the share capital to the amount of EUR35 000 within ten years after establishment.

[28] The company is represented by one or more managing directors, who are appointed by the shareholders and may be removed by the shareholders at any time without cause. The directors may be appointed for an indefinite time period and are directly bound to shareholders' instructions.

[29] The election of a supervisory board of directors is – except under certain circumstances – voluntary. The supervisory board is elected by the shareholders and consists of at least three members. Under certain conditions, it is obligatory that shareholders only elect two-thirds (but in any case, at least three) of the members of the supervisory board whereas the other third is elected by the employees, in order to protect their rights (co-determination, *see* 6.2.1).

[30] Shares of a limited liability company cannot be issued and a quotation on a stock exchange is not possible. A notarial transfer deed is required for a transfer of shares.

3.1.3 The Stock Corporation (*Aktiengesellschaft; AG*)

[31] The legal rules on stock corporations are primarily contained in the Stock Corporations Act. The main constitutional documents for the stock corporation are the Articles of Association (*Satzung*) which have to be notarized. The Articles of Association are filed with the commercial register upon registration of the company. The minimum share capital is EUR70 000, which may be paid up in cash or in kind. Shares are issued, and – under certain conditions – quotation on a stock exchange is possible.

[32] Austrian stock corporations are governed by a mandatory two-tier board system. The stock corporation is represented by the managing board of directors (*Vorstand*) who is appointed by the supervisory board for a maximum period of five years and is removable for important reasons only. In contrast to the limited liability company, the board members are not bound to the shareholders' orders, but only certain reserved matters require internal approval by the supervisory board of directors.

[33] A supervisory board of directors is mandatory. It is elected by the shareholders and consists of a minimum of three members. As with the limited liability company, the rules regarding the participation of employees in the supervisory board apply.

[34] General meetings of a stock corporation must be recorded by a notary public. Auditing is obligatory.

[35] Special rules apply for many corporate (governance) aspects in case of a listed stock corporation.

3.1.4 Commercial Partnerships

General Partnership (Offene Gesellschaft; OG)

[36] This form of enterprise is founded by two or more individuals or corporations, both of them endowed with full liability. The general partnership is represented by its partners. A partnership may incur liabilities, acquire assets and rights and may also be a party in lawsuits. General partnerships are governed by the Commercial Code.

Limited Partnership (Kommanditgesellschaft; KG)

[37] The limited partnership consists of two kinds of partners: at least one partner has full liability (*Komplementär*), the other partners (*Kommanditisten*) are liable up to the amount of their invested capital. The limited partnership is represented by its partner(s) with full liability. Just as the general partnership, limited partnerships may incur liabilities, acquire assets and rights and may also be a party in lawsuits. Limited partnerships are also governed by the Commercial Code.

3.1.5 Joint Ventures

[38] There are typically three different ways of concluding a joint venture:

(1) A joint venture company can be incorporated in the form of a stock corporation, a limited liability company or a commercial partnership to which the parties are shareholders or partners. The normal rules for corporations or partnerships – as described above – apply to this form of a joint venture.

(2) A joint venture can also be conducted by executing a co-operation agreement on a contractual basis. In this case, general contract law applies.

(3) The third typical way of concluding a joint venture is by forming a civil law partnership (*Gesellschaft bürgerlichen Rechts; GesbR*). This particular form is recommendable if the parties intend to work only on a narrowly defined project for a limited period of time since little administrative work is required to conduct a civil law partnership.

3.1.6 Subsidiaries and Branches

[39] Setting up a new branch of a non-resident foreign legal entity requires registration with the commercial register in order to complete its formal incorporation. In case of establishing a limited liability company or a stock corporation, enterprises residing in non-EU-Member States must appoint at least one representative whose habitual residence is in Austria.

[40] Disclosure of complete accounting records on all transactions carried out by the branch office of a foreign enterprise is obligatory.

[41] The decision of whether to establish a subsidiary or a branch office is often determined by tax considerations.

3.1.7 Publicly Available Information

[42] In Austria, the commercial register is the prime source of information about sole proprietors, commercial partnerships and corporations. It is established at the Regional Courts (*Landesgerichte*), in Vienna at the Commercial Court (*Handelsgericht*). The information available includes the registration number, name and address of the firm and the owners of a partnership or a company with limited liability, as well as the names of the persons authorized for representation and the starting date and nature of their power of representation. The files also contain financial statements as well as current and historical versions of the statutes. The register and the files attached are available to the public by electronic means.

[43] In addition to the commercial register, special gazettes (*Bekanntmachungsblätter*; *Wiener Zeitung*) provide the public with information such as copies of the financial statements and dates of general meetings. Furthermore, companies listed on a stock exchange have to comply with numerous information requirements and are obliged to publish certain information on their website.

3.2 Laws Affecting M&A

[44] In Austria, a private M&A acquisition is usually structured either as a purchase of shares in the target company (share deal) or of business assets (asset deal). In case of a share deal, the buyer directly acquires the shares in the target and (only) indirectly the target's business. The assets and liabilities pertaining to the business remain with the target. In case of an asset deal, the buyer acquires a business from a seller, which means that the assets and liabilities need to be moved from the seller to the buyer. Subject to limitations, in particular with respect to liabilities, the parties may further define the details of the scope of the purchased assets. Whether the one or other method is applied, often depends on tax considerations, but also on the scope, shape and complexity of the business that shall be acquired, liability issues, results of a due diligence and similar.

[45] If it is the intention to acquire shares in a stock corporation based in Austria the shares of which are admitted to trading on the Vienna Stock Exchange (*Wiener Börse*) on a regulated market, with the aim to obtain or expand the control in such listed company, a strictly regulated procedure must be followed, which is governed by the Austrian Takeover Act (*Übernahmegesetz*; *ÜbG*).

[46] In addition, alternative ways of acquisition are noteworthy, such as statutory mergers, either by absorption (one company is merged into another) or by combination (two companies are merged into a newly established company); however, these techniques are typically employed within a group of companies rather than among unaffiliated entities. Nevertheless, they may be employed as a preparatory step preceding a share deal with an unaffiliated entity in order to establish the envisaged target structure.

3.3 Relevant Regulatory Authorities

3.3.1 Merger Control

[47] The relevant authorities regarding merger control are the Federal Competition Authority (*Bundeswettbewerbsbehörde*), which is the recipient of Austrian merger control filings, the Federal Cartel Prosecutor (*Bundeskartellanwalt*) and the Cartel Court (*Kartellgericht*). Depending on the turnover thresholds, competence may pass to the European Commission, in which case the EU Merger Regulation exclusively applies without residual room for the Austrian merger control regime.

3.3.2 Dependent on Industry/Target Type

[48] Depending on the target entity's industry, regulators like the Financial Market Authority (*Finanzmarktaufsicht*) or E-Control, an authority monitoring the Austrian energy market, may supervise M&A activities and require additional notification obligations, approvals or 'fit and proper' tests (*see* 3.4.1 and 3.4.2). Such restrictions typically aim to assess the identity, quality and fitness of the new acquirer and are limited to regulated industries such as banking, insurance, investment, pensions, telecoms, aviation, gambling and in some respects, gas and power.

[49] Moreover, M&A activities within certain sensitive – mainly public order and safety related – industries may require an approval by the Austrian Ministry for Economic Affairs. Public takeovers of shares in Austrian-listed entities which fall within the Austrian Takeover Act are regulated and supervised by the Austrian Takeover Commission (*Übernahmekommission*).

3.3.3 Dependent on Asset Class

[50] Concerning real estate, acquisitions may, in some circumstances, be subject to notification or approval by regional land transfer authorities (*Grundverkehrsbehörde*) (*see* 3.4.1).

3.4 Foreign Investment

3.4.1 Controls and Restrictions on Foreign Investment

[51] Direct inward investments are usually freely possible. However, the following restrictions/authorization requirements are relevant to foreign investors.

Foreign Direct Investments (FDI)

[52] In Austria, the legislation on FDI screening is based on the Federal Act on the Control of Foreign Direct Investments (Investment Control Act – ICA) at the national level, which has been in force since 25 July 2020 (with the exception of the provisions on the cooperation mechanism at the EU level, which have been in force since 11 October 2020). Further, the Austrian Competition Act (*Wettbewerbsgesetz; WettbG*), which has been amended as of 10 September 2021, sees an obligation of the Austrian Federal Competition Authority to forward any merger notifications to the Austrian Ministry for Digital and Economic Affairs ('BMDW', which is responsible for FDI in Austria). Prior to the entry into force of the ICA, the control of foreign direct investments was regulated in section 25a Foreign Trade and Payments Act 2011 (*Außenwirtschaftsgesetz 2011 – AußWG 2011*).

[53] The ICA only applies to '*foreign*' direct investments (FDI) into 'Austrian companies'. Austrian companies are such that have their headquarters or at least a subsidiary in Austria. Based on the Austrian BMDW's current interpretation, a branch office (*Zweigniederlassung*) does not have the legal capacity and does not trigger an FDI filing requirement in Austria. An investment is 'foreign' if at least one acquirer does not have EU, EEA or Swiss nationality/headquarter or seat within the EU, EEA or Switzerland. Also, the ultimate controlling shareholders of the acquirers have to be considered for the assessment. Further, the BMDW interprets the term 'foreign' very broadly and has repeatedly taken the position that an investor is considered 'foreign' as soon as one company within a chain of controlling companies is domiciled outside the EU, EEA and Switzerland – even though ultimate control/beneficial ownership rests with an EU, EEA or Swiss company or individual. It remains to be seen whether the BMDW keeps this wide definition in the future.

[54] The Austrian target company to be acquired must be active in an area that is of particular importance for security or public order. FDI clearance is required if the transaction leads to the acquisition of a shareholding of at least 10% in an Austrian company active in an 'especially sensitive sector'. These are (1) defence equipment and technologies, (2) operation of critical energy infrastructure, (3) operation of critical digital infrastructure, in particular 5G infrastructure, (4) water, (5) operating systems guaranteeing the data sovereignty of the Republic of Austria and (6) research and development in the fields of pharmaceuticals, vaccines, medical devices and personal protective equipment. A clearance is also required if the transaction leads to the acquisition of a shareholding of at least 25% in (or (joint) control over) an Austrian company active in one of the 'other sensitive sectors' listed in the ICA. These are (i) critical infrastructure, (ii) critical technologies and dual-use goods as well as (iii) the security and supply of critical resources including, *inter alia*, energy, information technology, traffic and transport, health, food, telecommunications, data processing and storage, defence, constitutional institutions, finance, research institutions, social and distribution systems, artificial intelligence, robotics, semiconductors, cyber security, supply of raw materials etc. This list of sectors is not exhaustive. The BMDW may also consider other sectors to be relevant.

[55] An authorization is not required, if the Austrian target company is a 'microenterprise' (e.g. a start-up), with fewer than ten employees and an annual turnover or an annual balance sheet total of less than EUR 2 million.

[56] Furthermore, it is possible to apply for a clearance certificate prior to the acquisition process in order to clarify in advance whether the planned acquisition is subject to approval. This is highly recommended as the BMDW applies a very broad interpretation of the ICA and might consider sectors somehow related to the areas listed in paragraph [57] as suitable to trigger a notification requirement. In practice, the authority sometimes initiates proceedings ex officio if it considers that the transaction should have been notified (based on, e.g., publically available information, or an Austrian merger control notification which is automatically being forwarded to the BMDW). In such cases, the BMDW usually requests the parties involved to apply for clearance if it considers the transaction notifiable.

[57] Following receipt of the notification, the BMDW is required to inform the European Commission of the transaction without undue delay. The Commission and Member States of the European Union then have thirty-five calendar days to comment on the transaction. After the expiry of this deadline, the EU Commission may issue an opinion within a further five calendar days if the EU Member States have submitted comments. Within one month of the expiry of this period, the BMDW must either approve the transaction or initiate an in-depth investigation. The opening of an in-depth investigation triggers a further two-month (Phase 2) review period.

[58] The ICA provides for a prohibition to implement the transaction prior to clearance or expiry of the review periods due to inactivity. A transaction subject to a clearance requirement is not valid until the clearance is granted.

[59] The ICA provides for three types of sanctions for the implementation of a notifiable transaction without government approval: administrative (fines from up to EUR40 000), civil (nullity of the underlying legal transaction) and criminal (imprisonment of up to one year, in qualified cases up to three years). The criminal sanctions cover, *inter alia,* incorrect or incomplete information, gun-jumping and non-compliance with conditions in a (Phase II) clearance decision.

Aviation Industry

[60] Austrian aviation law requires an EEA/EU majority ownership in an Austrian airline company. If non-EEA or non-EU investors obtain control of an Austrian airline company, the operating licence may be revoked.

Media, Gas Pipes and Green Electricity Providers

[61] The licence of a radio broadcaster, media service provider or provider of gas pipes and green electricity providers may only be issued to Austrian or EEA/EU citizens or companies having their seat in Austria or in the EEA/EU. The competent regulatory authority must be informed of any change of ownership of such companies and may, in the case of major changes in the ownership (e.g., more than 50% of the shares in the case of a radio broadcaster or a media service provider), scrutinize whether the requirements for obtaining a licence are still fulfilled.

Real Estate

[62] The acquisition of real estate assets by foreign (non-EEA) investors may be subject to notification or approval by regional land transfer authorities (*Grundverkehrsbehörde*). Since this matter is regulated by each Austrian federal province individually, different provisions apply depending on where the respective real estate is located, which type of real estate is involved and whether the acquisition may be triggered by an asset deal or also by a share deal or even by an indirect change of control in a company which owns the property.

Money Laundering & Dealings with Blacklisted States and Individuals

[63] Further restrictions may arise from anti-money laundering legislation and KYC requirements, as well as in relation to intended transactions with blacklisted/sanctioned foreign states and/or individuals.

3.4.2 Controls and Restrictions Equally Relevant for Austrian Investors

Banking/Insurance/Gambling Industry and Pension Funds

[64] Acquisitions in the banking or insurance industry and pension funds require the passing of certain 'fit and proper' tests which apply to significant shareholders, depending on certain thresholds of shareholdings, e.g.:

- 10%, 20%, 30%, respectively 33% and 50% of the voting rights or of the share capital of the respective company in the case of financial institutions; or
- similar thresholds in the case of insurance companies, pension funds and green electricity providers.

[65] The rules concerning shareholdings in the gambling industry are even stricter; the prior consent of the competent authority is necessary regardless of any thresholds.

[66] Change of ownership in the Austrian target will, therefore, usually require advance notification to the respective regulatory authority, which could then block the acquisition. In such case, the transfer of the shares should be conditional upon the approval of the respective authority. Such consent of the respective authority is, in various cases, deemed to be given if the acquisition is not prohibited within a certain period of time. The consequences of not fulfilling these regulatory legal requirements may range from denial of registration of the acquisition (e.g., in the case of acquisitions in financial institutions) to the suspension of any voting rights (in the case of acquisitions in pension funds).

Alternative Investment Funds

[67] Alternative Investment Funds managers managing alternative investment funds which acquire control (i.e., a majority of voting rights) of non-listed companies and issuers, with the exception of small- and medium-sized companies and real estate special purpose vehicles, are subject to certain notification and disclosure obligations (regarding among other things certain shareholding thresholds) and asset stripping restrictions.

3.4.3 Incentives for Foreign Investment

General

[68] The federal, provincial and municipal governments may encourage foreign investment by granting either cash, subsidies or other kinds of benefits to investors depending, however, on the availability of subsidy programmes. Such subsidies may typically be obtained if an investment is beneficial to the state, its economy or its attractiveness as a business location for both investors and the labour force. Subsidies may also be granted for certain innovation and technology projects.

[69] Furthermore, tax incentives – most of which are granted in the form of tax exemptions – have been granted to investors in the past. Foreign investors also took advantage of export incentives offered by the state.

(Currency) Exchange Control

[70] The Austrian Central Bank (*Österreichische Nationalb*ank; *OeNB*) administers the exchange control system under the Foreign Exchange Act (*Devisengesetz 2004*) and is appointed to regulate all foreign exchange transactions. The Austrian Central Bank is authorized to issue general regulations, by which it usually grants its approval to specific kinds of transactions. This system allows for swift adjustment to the applicable legal framework, if required by changes in the international or national financial environment.

[71] The Austrian foreign exchange system for transactions has been liberalized in accordance with European law resulting in extensive facilitation for the average business person. With the exception of certain cases referred to in the Treaty on the Functioning of the European Union (TFEU), capital and payment transactions with foreign countries are not subject to any restrictions. However, insofar as the

Council of the EU adopts measures pursuant to the respective Articles of the TFEU, the Austrian Central Bank is obliged to take the necessary steps to implement such measures vis-à-vis the non-EU country concerned. Furthermore, in order to fulfil obligations under international law or to safeguard Austria's foreign interests, the Austrian Central Bank may, unless directly applicable European law precludes it, take measures necessary to restrict the movement of capital and payments in accordance with section 4 of the Foreign Exchange Act.

[72] However, exchange regulations are frequently altered by the Austrian Central Bank; therefore, it is advisable to demand updated information from Austrian credit institutions. Particularly in case of complex transactions, the assistance of a legal counsel is recommended, since the Foreign Exchange Act entails grave sanctions for violations.

[73] Exceptions to the general approval for all business transactions concern accounts of Austrians abroad, banking transactions, and credit and loan transactions. In certain cases, notification requirements need to be considered. There are no restrictions in Austria concerning the purchase and exchange of foreign currency into European currency.

[74] The regulations under the Austrian Income Tax concerning dividends are valid for foreign shareholders without any difference. Income repatriation does not generate any exchange control related taxes, fees or duties of any kind. Payment of employees, suppliers and others is not subject to any exchange regulations; it can also be carried out in foreign currency. However, labour law rules might provide that payments by an Austrian company – whether it is a subsidiary or branch of a foreign entity – to its employees have to be effected in local currency.

3.5 Specific Issues of Company Law

3.5.1 Shareholder Approval

Asset Deals

[75] If a limited liability company or stock corporation sells all or almost all of its assets, a shareholders' resolution is required. In this case, approval by 75% of the shareholders or by a higher quorum set by the articles of association has to be obtained. Without such resolution, the asset purchase agreement's validity itself is affected.

Legal Mergers

[76] Austrian corporate law allows mergers between two or more limited liability companies and two or more stock corporations, as well as mergers of stock corporations into limited liability companies and vice versa. Two forms of mergers apply:

(1) the transferring company is merged into an existing company, with the shareholders of the transferring company receiving shares in the receiving company as compensation (absorption); or
(2) a NewCo is formed to which all the assets and liabilities of two or more corporations are transferred, with the shareholders of all these companies receiving shares in NewCo (consolidation).

[77] The transferring companies are dissolved by law and their assets and liabilities are transferred in a single act into the receiving company (universal succession).

[78] The merger contract must be approved by the shareholders' meeting of all companies participating in the merger by a 75% majority vote of the share capital represented at the meeting. The articles of association of the respective corporations may prescribe a higher quorum or additional requirements. For stock corporations with more than one share class, additional separate votes must be taken for each share class.

[79] As regards limited liability companies, the Limited Liability Companies Act provides for detailed additional consent requirements relating to shareholders with special rights, which, among other things, may relate to the right to participate in the management or nominate a manager of the company or their consent requirement to share transfers. In certain cases, e.g., where the contributions are not fully paid in, the unanimous vote of the shareholders of the acquiring limited liability company is needed, as shareholders are subject to the residual payment obligations under section 70 of the Limited Liability Companies Act. Such consents must be given in the shareholders' meeting, recorded in a notarial protocol, or given in writing with notarized or court-certified signatures.

[80] No shareholders' resolution of the receiving company is required in case of a 'simplified merger' pursuant to section 231 paragraph 1 of the Stock Corporations Act, provided that:

- 90% or more of the transferring company's shares are held by the receiving company (except where at least 5% of the shareholders of the receiving company demand such a resolution); or
- the total nominal value of the shares to be issued does not exceed 10% of the receiving company's (increased) share capital.

[81] Another, further simplified, merger is feasible under section 232 of the Stock Corporations Act if the receiving company is the direct or indirect sole shareholder of the transferring company. In this case, certain items in the merger contract may be omitted and there is no requirement for a shareholders' meeting and resolution for the transferring company neither.

Demergers

[82] Stock corporations and limited liability companies may split their assets under the rules of the Austrian Demerger Act (*Spaltungsgesetz*; *SpaltG*). The law provides for two types of demergers: the split-up (*Aufspaltung*) and the spin-off (*Abspaltung*).

[83] In the course of a split-up, the transferring company is dissolved without liquidation and transfers all its assets and liabilities in a single act to an existing (*Aufspaltung zur Aufnahme*) and/or newly formed company or companies (*Aufspaltung zur Neugründung*). The shareholders of the transferring company surrender their shares and receive new shares of such existing and/or newly formed companies.

[84] In the course of a spin-off, one or more assets of a company are transferred in a single act to existing (receiving) companies (*Abspaltung zur Aufnahme*) or newly formed companies (*Abspaltung zur Neugründung*), with the company transferring the assets being continued with its remaining assets.

[85] In consideration of the transfer of the assets, the shareholders of the transferring company receive shares in the NewCo and/or the receiving company.

[86] A demerger requires a notarized shareholders' resolution with a 75% majority vote in each company participating in the demerger (as transferring or receiving company). The articles of association of the companies involved may prescribe a higher quorum or additional requirements. Where a stock corporation is involved, special resolutions must be taken for different share categories (if any). For limited liability companies, the holders of special rights must consent.

[87] Where there is a change in the respective shareholder ratios (*nicht verhältniswahrende Spaltung*), the shareholders' resolution requires a 90% majority of the total nominal share capital issued. If such a majority is not achieved, the resolution is valid only if the receiving company is supplied with notarized or court-certified consent declarations of a sufficient number of shareholders to reach the required 90% majority within three months from the date of the resolution.

[88] An approval by all shareholders is required if:

- the shares in a company are only or predominantly allocated to shareholders with a total stake of not more than 10%; or
- a cash box structure is implemented.

3.5.2 Director's Duties

[89] Austrian stock corporations are governed by a two-tier board system. The same applies to limited liability companies in case a supervisory board has been established. The members of both boards, management board and supervisory board are required to comply with the duty of care of a prudent businessman (*Sorgfalt eines ordentlichen Geschäftsleiters*) and act foremost in the best interest of the company. Additionally, but only ranking second, shareholders', employees' and public interests may be taken into consideration. Besides that, section 47a of the Austrian

Stock Corporation Act states a general principle of equal treatment of all shareholders.

[90] Subject to the principles of the so-called business judgement rule, a failure to comply with these duties may result in personal liability. The business judgment rule, as it is understood in Austria, establishes a 'safe harbour' with regard to decisions of board members, provided that:

- a business decision is made;
- the board members act free from conflicts of interest;
- the decision is based on all information reasonably available; and
- the board members have justifiably believed that the decision was in the best interest of the company.

[91] A board member acting within the scope of the business judgement rule will generally not be liable to the company, its shareholders or its other stakeholders. However, the business judgement rule will not help if the law explicitly sets up a more specific rule in certain situations. Violations of law, even if they were believed to be in the best interest of the company, cannot be justified under the business judgment rule.

[92] In connection with M&A activities, the directors' duties of care and loyalty are not differing from those in other business situations. The influence of directors of a target, particularly in a share deal, is limited since negotiations are conducted, and decisions are made, typically at the shareholder level. In some cases, target companies' managing directors are not even involved at an early stage. However, in order to provide information, their involvement is usually required in the due diligence process and in connection with the closing.

[93] The Austrian Takeover Act additionally requires managing directors as well as members of the supervisory board to act in the interest of all shareholders as well as in the interest of the employees, creditors and the general public, and to remain objective during the takeover procedure (*see* paragraph [152] below).

3.5.3 Form of Consideration for Issuance of Shares

[94] Subscribing shareholders usually pay cash to a company in return for the issuance of shares. However, the Limited Liability Companies Act and the Stock Corporations Act allow for the company issuing shares to accept as consideration a contribution in kind instead of cash – always provided, however, that the strict company law provisions on capital contribution and prohibition on dilution of shares are complied with. The contribution in kind may be either a single asset, a group of assets, an entire business or a branch.

[95] A contribution in kind of assets constitutes sufficient payment for the issuance of shares typically only if the following conditions are complied with.

[96] The shareholders' resolution on the capital increase must include a description of the contribution in kind and the nominal value of the share capital issued as consideration; the resolution is valid only if the non-cash contribution was included and properly described in the invitation to the shareholders' meeting.

[97] The value of the contribution in kind must be audited by an outside certified public accountant who is appointed by the court, and such certified public accountant's report must be filed with the court. If the certified public accountant's report indicates that the value of the non-cash contribution is below the nominal value of the new share capital issued in return, registration of the capital increase in the commercial register will be denied.

[98] If it is demonstrated after registration of the capital increase that the value of the contribution in kind did not equal the increase in share capital issued, the subscribing shareholder is personally liable for the difference in cash.

3.5.4 Capital Maintenance

[99] Austrian corporate law has very strict rules on capital maintenance, essentially protecting the entire assets of an Austrian company against (hidden) repayment or retransfer to the direct or indirect shareholders or side-stream affiliates. Therefore, any transactions, payments or other value shifts (with the exception of the formal annual distribution of balance sheet profits or a formal decrease of a company's registered share capital) which is not made on arm's length terms but to the detriment of the company (i.e., whenever the company does not receive adequate arm's length consideration) violates Austrian capital maintenance rules.

[100] Consequently, in case an acquisition is financed by bank loans, members of the target group would be prohibited to provide the bank with collateral to secure loans made to the acquiring company whenever the respective member of the target group does not receive adequate arm's length consideration.

[101] Benefits made to future shareholders with regard to their future shareholder status are also prohibited. Therefore, the financial assistance given by a company for the purchase of its own shares would constitute a violation of Austrian capital maintenance rules.

[102] The consequences of such violation are:

- the nullity of the respective contract or transaction;
- the right of the company to reclaim compensation of the value that has been illicitly drained/shifted from the company;
- the possible personal civil law liability of the managing directors involved in such contract or transaction; and
- under certain circumstances, even the possible criminal law liability of the managing directors involved in such contract or transaction.

[103] Furthermore, any such intragroup transactions which are not at arm's length terms but to the benefit of a direct or indirect shareholder or sister entity may also qualify as 'hidden profit distribution' under applicable tax regimes. Any intragroup transaction that is not compliant with arm's length terms may also raise transfer pricing issues under the applicable tax regimes (*see* 5.4.3).

3.5.5 Completion Formalities

Transfer of Shares

[104] A transfer of shares but also any obligation or commitment to transfer shares in a limited liability company requires a notarial deed. The articles of association of a limited liability company may impose restrictions on transferability, such as requiring the prior consent of the company or other shareholders, or pre-emptive rights for other shareholders. The limited liability company must be informed of the transfer to allow the new shareholders to exercise their rights against the company. The transfer is completed by registration of the new shareholders in the commercial register.

[105] The transfer of shares in a stock corporation does not require a notarial deed. Stock corporation shares may be bearer or registered shares. However, the freedom of choice is limited, since only listed companies, or companies intending to become listed, can issue bearer shares. Registered shares (including shares evidenced by interim certificates) are transferred by endorsement or assignment. The articles of association may provide for shareholder consent requirements for registered shares but not for bearer shares. The acquirer of registered shares may exercise the rights in the shares vis-à-vis the stock corporation only upon notification to the stock corporation of the acquisition and the registration of the acquirer in the stock corporation's share ledger. In relation to bearer shares, a deposit receipt from the bank is sufficient for the exercise of shareholder rights.

Transfer of Assets

[106] Austrian corporate law and civil law do not contain a comprehensive set of norms relating to the acquisition of a business as a going concern. Every single asset must be transferred pursuant to the respective civil and commercial law provisions applicable to allow a valid transfer of such an asset:

- Tangible movable assets are transferred by way of a transfer agreement and physical delivery (or some form of surrogate).
- Real property is transferred by way of a transfer agreement and registration of the transfer in the land register (*Grundbuch*).
- Limited liability company shares belonging to the business are transferred by way of a transfer agreement in the form of a notarial deed.
- For the transfer of trademarks notarization of signatures on trademark assignment deeds is required.
- Third-party consent will usually be required to transfer contracts. In the case of the transfer of a business as a going concern, section 38 of the Commercial Code simplifies the transfer of contracts pertaining thereto, including the individual rights and liabilities having emerged therefrom, to the extent that the transfer occurs automatically unless the relevant third party, having been duly notified, has vetoed the transfer of its contract within a three-month period.

- Employment contracts, certain insurance contracts and certain tenancy rights will be transferred automatically to the new owner.
- In the case of a lease, the lessor must be notified, to allow the lessor (in defined cases) to increase below-market rent to current market level.

[107] Civil and commercial law set forth rules for the liability on the purchase of a business for debts, which have been incurred by the business before the transfer (so-called old debts). Exclusion of the acquirer's liability for such old debts is only partially possible. Special rules apply to liability for social security contributions and taxes.

3.5.6 Dividends

[108] In general, dividends can only be paid out of distributable balance sheet profits for the year as shown in the annual financial statements. Since the annual financial statements are not drawn up until after the end of the financial year and the entitlement to a dividend is conditional upon the approval of the annual financial statements, shareholders can typically only assert their claim to profits around the middle of the next financial year.

[109] However, section 54a of the Stock Corporations Act provides that the management board, with the approval of the supervisory board, may, after half of the financial year has passed, pay the shareholders an accrual on the expected balance sheet profit of up to half of the average annual dividend for the last three years, provided that these discount payments are covered by the result of the past half of the financial year determined on the basis of an interim balance sheet plus any profit carried forward and less any loss carried forward. Furthermore, distributable reserves in the equivalent amount of the amounts paid out must remain.

3.5.7 Purchase of Own Shares

[110] The acquisition of own shares by a stock corporation is limited to certain narrow circumstances. These circumstances include:

- protection of the company from serious, imminent damage;
- acquisition to offer the shares to employees and to management under a stock purchase or stock option plan within thirty months;
- acquisition to use the shares to satisfy legal compensation claims of minority shareholders;
- acquisition for no consideration;
- acquisition by universal succession; and
- in the case of stock corporations, the shares of which are listed, the repurchase of shares on the basis of an authorization by the shareholders' meeting which may be given for a maximum period of thirty months.

[111] In some cases, the total nominal amount of own shares that may be acquired by the company is limited to 10% of the company's stated share capital. These restrictions also apply to the purchase of shares in a parent corporation by its directly or indirectly owned subsidiary and the acquisition for the account of the parent or subsidiary. Treasury shares (shares which are held by the stock corporation itself or its subsidiaries) are non-voting and carry no dividend or subscription rights.

[112] In detail, the rules on the purchase of own shares in stock corporations are fairly complex and differ in detail according to the reasons (see above) for which the share repurchase is being implemented.

[113] In a limited liability company, the acquisition of own shares and their acceptance as a pledge are prohibited and unenforceable. However, the acquisition of own shares by execution in order to secure receivables of the company is allowed. Concerning an acquisition for no consideration, an acquisition by universal succession and an acquisition to use the shares to satisfy legal compensation claims of minority shareholders, the rules of the Stock Corporations Act apply (section 81 of the Limited Liability Companies Act).

3.5.8 The Corporate Veil

[114] Companies limited by shares have a separate legal personality, wholly distinct from that of their members. The assets of the company are separate from those of its shareholders. In principle, only the company assets are liable for the company's liabilities, not the private assets of the shareholders.

[115] In very limited circumstances, shareholders may be made liable for the company's liabilities (piercing of the corporate veil). However, these cases are highly controversial in legal literature.

Commingling of Assets (Vermögensvermischung)

[116] The principle that the assets of the company are separate from those of its shareholders is violated if the assets of the company are commingled in such a way that they can no longer be separated from those of the shareholders, so that it is also no longer discernible whether an unlawful transfer of assets from the company to a shareholder has taken place or not. The rationale for the shareholder's liability in such case is seen in the fact that the strict capital maintenance rules, which are a trade-off for a shareholder's limited liability, are no longer effective when the separation of asset spheres is rendered impossible. The Supreme Court (*Oberste Gerichtshof*; *OGH*) has recognized the shareholder's liability arising out of the commingling of assets.

Commingling of Spheres (Sphärenvermischung)

[117] The commingling of spheres refers to cases in which it is no longer clear whether the shareholder represents himself or, rather, the company in a specific matter. Examples of such a mixture of spheres include, in particular, the management of similar firms or business addresses, the use of the same business premises and the employment of the same personnel.

[118] However, in our view, the commingling of spheres should not constitute a case of the piercing of the corporate veil but shall be judged instead according to the rules of the right of representation.

Destroying the Existence of the Company

[119] In Germany, a shareholder may be held personally liable for detrimental interference with the company's affairs, which leads to the company's insolvency, in exceptional cases. However, the Supreme Court has not classified the destroying of the existence of the company as a case of the piercing of the corporate veil so far but has judged the destroying of the existence of the company under damages (tort law) principles.

Gross Undercapitalization

[120] The liability of a shareholder may also be considered if the company is clearly insufficiently equipped with equity capital in relation to the volume of business making it very likely that the creditors may suffer damages.

[121] The Supreme Court seems to accept such liability in principle but has never used the theory of gross undercapitalization as a basis for the liability of a shareholder so far.

Misuse of the Corporation's Legal Structure

[122] The Supreme Court is considering the misuse of the corporation's legal structure as a case of the piercing of the corporate veil, without specifying its prerequisites in further detail.

[123] Under this category, part of the Austrian doctrine considers cases of artificial splitting of a single undertaking into numerous companies and the transfer of risky transactions to a separate company. The creditors of this company would be considerably disadvantaged compared to the creditors of the other companies.

De Facto Director (faktischer Geschäftsführer)

[124] Note that shareholders may be liable under tort law under certain circumstances. This may especially be the case if a shareholder exercises significant influence on the management of the company, acting as a de facto director, even though he has not actually been appointed managing director, and thereby damages creditors.

[125] Furthermore, shareholders may be liable in case they have instructed the managing directors to refrain from initiating a reorganization procedure if so required by the Company Reorganization Act (*Unternehmensreorganisationsgesetz*; *URG*), or if they have not agreed to a proposal to initiate such a procedure.

[126] In addition, shareholders may be liable if they cause the managing directors not to apply for the opening of insolvency proceedings or not to apply for such proceedings without undue delay, even though the requirements are met.

3.5.9 Choice of Jurisdiction

[127] Disputes arising from international contracts can be brought before the place of jurisdiction of the defendant, as to say, at the place of domicile of the defendant. According to section 66 paragraph 2 of the Law on Jurisdiction (*Jurisdiktionsnorm*; *JN*) (outside of the application of the Brussels Ia Regulation), even the habitual residence of a party may justify jurisdiction of the respective Austrian court.

[128] The parties also have the option to choose the competent court for a particular dispute. The permissibility of such choice of jurisdiction clauses is to be assessed upon the relevant law, in Austria upon Article 25 of the Brussels Ia Regulation and in respect of purely domestic cases according to section 104 of the Law on Jurisdiction. Agreements about the place of jurisdiction have to be done in written form and have to be signed by the parties.

[129] If one party to an agreement is a consumer (a person concluding a contract for a purpose which is outside of his trade or profession; the private purpose of the owned performance has to be objectively recognizable), the Brussels Ia Regulation provide for special rules which warrant the consumer a place of jurisdiction at the place of his residence. Furthermore, section 14 of the Austrian Consumer Protection Act (*Konsumentenschutzgesetz*; *KSchG*) states that in case of the consumer having his place of domicile or work place within Austria, only the jurisdiction of a court situated in the district of such domicile or place of work can be agreed upon between the parties.

3.5.10 Choice of Law

[130] The Rome I Regulation applies to contractual obligations involving a choice between the laws of different countries and partly replaces the Austrian International Private Law Act (*Internationales Privatrechts-Gesetz*; *IPRG*) in the field of contractual obligations unless otherwise provided. Article 1 paragraph 2 Rome I excludes certain fields of the international contract law (i.e., questions involving the status or legal capacity of natural persons; arbitration agreements and agreements on the choice of court; questions governed by the law of companies and other bodies corporate or unincorporate; the question whether an agent is able to bind a principal, or an organ to bind a company or body corporate or unincorporate, to a third party; the constitution of trusts and the relationship between settlers, trustees and beneficiaries; evidence and procedure; contracts of insurance which cover risks situated in the territories of the Member States).

[131] The Convention is characterized by the principle of the parties' freedom to choose the applicable law, just as the Austrian International Private Law Act. This means that the contract shall be governed by the law chosen by the parties. The choice of law must be expressed or demonstrated with reasonable certainty by the terms of the contract or circumstances of the case. The chosen law can be either applied to the whole or only to a certain part of the contract. However, the choice of law may be displaced by mandatory rules of another relevant jurisdiction (e.g., in case of an employment contract choice of law shall not deprive the employee of the protection of mandatory rules of the law which would otherwise have governed the employment agreement) or may be inapplicable for reasons of the public policy of the law of the country in which proceedings are brought.

[132] Furthermore, a choice of law made by the parties shall not have the result of depriving the consumer of the protection granted to him by the mandatory rules of the law of the country in which he has his habitual residence.

3.5.11 Arbitration Practice

[133] Arbitration courts (*Schiedsgerichte*) in Austria are typically intended to offer time and cost-efficient settlements of civil and trade law disputes. The Austrian Code of Civil Procedure (*Zivilprozessordnung*; *ZPO*) provides for the settlement of disputes arising out of or in connection with a contract by arbitration only if the parties have agreed to submit the dispute to arbitration by prior written agreement.

[134] Arbitration agreements between an entrepreneur and a consumer can only be effectively concluded for disputes that have already arisen. Furthermore, arbitration agreements involving a consumer must be contained in a document signed by the consumer himself. Agreements other than those relating to arbitration may not be included in such document.

[135] Like in most other industrial countries, civil and trade law disputes are frequently settled by arbitration, often under the Rules of Arbitration of the International Chamber of Commerce or the Vienna International Arbitral Centre's Rules of Arbitration. Both institutional arbitration and ad hoc arbitration are possible. In the latter case, arbitration frequently happens before a panel of three arbitrators. The defendant and plaintiff parties each nominate one arbitrator, and the chairman is selected by these two arbitrators.

[136] Arbitral awards are enforceable, just like other court judgments. Only in certain cases, an arbitral award can be challenged in courts of law. That is, if:

- there is no valid arbitration agreement (an arbitration agreement must be made in written form and must describe precisely the nature of the disputes to be referred to arbitration);
- a party was not given proper notice of the appointment of an arbitrator or was otherwise not able to present its case;
- the constitution or composition of the arbitral tribunal is not in accordance with the provisions of the Austrian Code of Civil Procedure or with a valid agreement of the parties;
- the arbitration proceedings were conducted in a way so as to violate Austrian public policy;
- the preconditions for a retrial are satisfied (e.g., when the award was obtained by forged documents, perjury or sworn false testimony or through other crimes);
- the arbitrators exceeded their legal authorities;
- the arbitral award violates Austrian public policy.

[137] It has to be mentioned that the option of disputing an arbitral award cannot be waived. Nevertheless, disputing an arbitral award is only possible after the arbitrators have rendered a decision.

3.6 Public Takeovers

3.6.1 Preparation

Stake Building

[138] Although acquiring an initial stake in a listed target company prior to launching a public offer is generally permitted under Austrian takeover law, a shareholder is under an obligation to fulfil certain notification requirements if the thresholds described below are met or exceeded. As a consequence, stake building involves the risk of generating publicity.

[139] The amendment of Directive 2004/109/EC of the European Parliament and of the Council on the harmonization of transparency requirements in 2013 introduced stricter disclosure requirements, including, for instance, a reporting obligation regarding cash-settled equity swaps, which makes it harder to carry out a creeping increase of control over a listed company.

[140] Under section 130 of the Austrian Stock Exchange Act (*Börsegesetz 2018*; *BörseG 2018*), any person directly or indirectly acquiring or selling shares in a company listed on a regulated market is required to inform the Austrian Financial Market Authority and the exchange operating company if their shares carrying voting rights reach, exceed or fall below the thresholds of 4%, 5%, 10%, 15%, 20%, 25%, 30%, 35%, 40%, 45%, 50%, 75% and 90%.

[141] These material shareholding disclosure thresholds only apply to shareholders who hold an interest in a company whose registered office is in Austria. The personal scope of application includes individuals, legal persons, registered partnerships without legal personality, and investment funds. The aim of the provision is to ensure the functioning of the capital market and to provide a reliable basis for shareholders concerning decisions about the acquisition and sale of shares.

Due Diligence

[142] In the course of takeovers, due diligence is rather the exception than the rule. In such cases, the scope of due diligence would usually focus on publicly available information of the target (*see* 3.1.7). However, given that Austrian-listed entities often have a shareholder structure with one (or few) core shareholders holding a majority stake, and comparatively moderate free float, a public takeover is often combined with, or triggered by, a share package deal with such core shareholder(s), who may be able to offer quite substantial information and insight in the target company as part of a due diligence process (subject to confidentiality undertakings), thus in many cases enabling a due diligence with a usual (although frequently limited and high level) scope of the target entity as part of such share package acquisition.

Deal Security

[143] The principle of freedom of contract granted by Austrian law enables transaction parties to seek any type of deal security measure as long as they do not violate moral principles (*Sittenwidrigkeit*). However, in situations where the Austrian Takeover Act applies, further limitations need to be observed.

[144] Exclusivity agreements are quite commonly sought after by a bidder from a core shareholder and should be legally feasible, particularly in a phase preceding a public offer, but arguably also during a tender process. Exclusivity arrangements with the target, however, appear more problematic, in particular, if they are aimed to restrict the free business judgment of management acting in the best interest of all shareholders. Therefore, no-talk arrangements (lock-ups) typically risk being too restrictive and thus void, while there are good arguments that no shop provisions and market test provisions (if they just limit management to actively look for other bidders) are more likely to be upheld.

[145] Break-up fees will be in conflict with the Austrian Takeover Act if the amounts involved are substantial so that they de facto exclude or materially impede competing offers (in particular, if they are not limited to just compensating the bidder for its out-of-pocket costs but also have some penalty element).

[146] Standstill obligations are essentially already foreseen by the Austrian Takeover Act containing statutory rules prohibiting the launch of a new or modified offer once the tender offer is published (with only very few exceptions) as well as a statutory waiting period in case the offer turns out to be unsuccessful.

[147] The shareholder structure of Austrian-listed companies is typically composed of one or a few core shareholders holding large share packages, whereas the percentage of free float shares is sometimes rather limited. Therefore, it is not uncommon to approach – if it makes sense strategically – a core shareholder first and to privately negotiate and seek an irrevocable commitment by such shareholder to sell his shares before launching a public offer. There are good arguments supporting the validity of such commitments even with a view of a public tender process and it might also be argued (although some grey area exists) that such irrevocable commitment, if already made prior to the launch of a public tender offer, should remain binding also in case of a competing offer.

[148] Contractual provisions providing an option for the principal shareholder to withdraw such commitment before a tender process is initiated, in our experience, rather unusual, although such clause would seem legally possible. Within a tender process, the Austrian Takeover Act gives shareholders, who have already accepted a public tender offer, the mandatory right to withdraw their acceptance in the event a competing tender offer is launched (but a contractual right of exit will make sense for those commitments which – as outlined above – would otherwise arguably remain binding in a subsequent tender process).

3.6.2 The Austrian Takeover Act

General

[149] Generally speaking, the Austrian Takeover Act regulates public offers aimed at obtaining or expanding control by acquiring shares issued by a stock corporation with its registered seat in Austria and the shares of which are listed on a regulated market on the Vienna Stock Exchange. Furthermore, the Austrian Takeover Act also (partially) applies where only the requirement of a registered seat or the listing is fulfilled in Austria and the respective other requirement is fulfilled in another jurisdiction.

[150] Section 3 of the Austrian Takeover Act sets forth the following general principles:

- Equal treatment of all stockholders of a target company who are in the same position.
- The stockholders must be protected when control is acquired over a company.
- The addressees of a bid must have sufficient time and adequate information to make an informed decision.
- The management and supervisory board of the target company must act in the best interests of all shareholders or other holders of equities, employees, creditors as well as in the public interest.
- False statements must be avoided.
- The takeover must be conducted quickly; in particular, a takeover bid must not impede the business activities of the target company beyond a reasonable period of time.

[151] The Austrian Takeover Act establishes the Takeover Commission (*Übernahmekommission*) as the supervisory authority, which is competent to decide on all matters concerning the Austrian Takeover Act.

Protective Actions

[152] The Austrian Takeover Act requires managing directors as well as members of the supervisory board to act in the interest of all shareholders as well as in the interest of the employees, creditors and the general public, and to remain objective during the takeover procedure. As soon as the intention to launch a bid has been announced, but also when the members of the boards have been approached by a bidder or have knowledge of the intention to launch a bid, the boards must not prevent the public bid (*Verhinderungsverbot*), must stay objective (*Objektivitätsgebot*) and, in addition, have to respond to the bid by way of a statement.

[153] Therefore, only a very limited selection of protective actions is available to the managing directors of a target company, which may be divided into prophylactic measures and measures taken after an intention to make an offer has been announced.

Prophylactic Measures

[154] Even though it is more feasible to take prophylactic measures than to take measures after an intention to make an offer has been announced, there is still only a rather limited selection available. Prophylactic measures may be, e.g., changes in the structure of the target company intending to create stability within the decision-making process, the shareholders and governance (e.g., maximum numbers of votes; restrictions on share transferability; staggered terms for the board of directors and/or the supervisory board; a higher quorum for the removal of directors; the definition of necessary personal qualifications of directors).

[155] The possibility of the target company to prophylactically purchase its own shares is rather limited (*see* 3.5.7).

[156] Also, the possibility to dilute the bidders' shareholdings is rather limited due to the pro rata subscription right, which entitles existing shareholders in the case of an increase in share capital to subscribe for a portion of the new shares issued equal to their existing participation in the company's capital prior to the increase.

[157] A flip-in provision incorporated in the articles of association of the target company, giving the current shareholders the right to subscribe to additional shares in the target company in the case of a hostile bidder's acquiring a certain threshold of shares, may be executed only in the course of a formal share capital increase. Such capital increase is, first, dependent on the general assembly's approval, and second, the hostile bidder may be excluded from this preemptive right only for sufficiently justified reasons. However, in the case of so-called authorized capital (*genehmigtes Kapital*), the managing board has, within the limitations set by the shareholder's meeting and the law, some freedom to decide on whether in which amount and when to implement a share capital increase.

[158] Finally, the interest of a potential hostile bidder in the target company may deteriorate if the target company has the option to dispose of essential assets (i.e., the crown jewels) to a third party.

Measures Taken after an Intention to Make an Offer Has Been Announced

[159] After the bidder's intention to make an offer has been announced, only rather few defensive measures remain available, which may only be taken under very limited circumstances and require the approval of the shareholders' meeting in any event. Under certain circumstances, it may be considered to take measures such as the inclusion of change of control clauses in certain contracts, the issuance of securities, the purchase or disposal of own shares, the disposal of important assets of the company, or significant changes concerning the company's finance structure. Furthermore, the managing directors may search for a 'white knight' to make a competing offer.

[160] In addition, any decisions of the management board or supervisory board (e.g., decisions regarding prophylactic measures) which have not yet been fully implemented until the time at which the target company becomes aware of the bidder's intention to make a bid, also require the approval of the shareholder's meeting if such measures are not part of routine business procedures and if their implementation might frustrate the bid.

Types of Offers

[161] The Austrian Takeover Act distinguishes between three types of offers, namely mandatory offers, voluntary offers and voluntary offers aimed at obtaining control. Furthermore, as of 3 January 2018, a new section has been introduced to the Austrian Takeover Act, which governs offers for delisting securities from the

Official Market of the Vienna Stock Exchange. Such offers are subject to the provisions governing mandatory offers whereby certain modifications apply.

[162] The obligation to launch a mandatory offer is triggered if a bidder (any individual or parties acting in concert) acquires a controlling interest in a target company. However, this obligation does not apply if the shareholding in the target company does not convey a controlling influence over it or if the legal entity exercising such influence does not change when taking into account the 'substance over form' approach.

[163] A 'controlling interest' is obtained by acquiring a direct or indirect shareholding in a target company, which represents more than 30% of the voting rights attached to the shares with permanent voting rights. If the bidder, or parties acting in concert, may exercise direct or indirect influence on the exercise of voting rights by third parties, the respective shares are attributed to the bidder.

[164] The Austrian Takeover Act also regulates the so-called creeping in by shareholders. If a shareholder obtains a controlling interest, which does, however, not provide them with the majority of the voting rights, and within one calendar year obtains at least an additional 3% of the voting rights, compared to the last day of the preceding calendar year a mandatory offer must be launched.

[165] Although no obligation to launch a mandatory offer is triggered, the acquisition of a shareholding between 26% and 30% of the voting rights must be notified to the Austrian Takeover Commission immediately but at the latest within twenty trading days as of acquisition of the shares. In this case, it shall not be possible to exercise more than 26% of the voting rights unless another shareholder (together with any parties acting in concert) holds at least as many voting rights in the target company as the concerned equity holder, or if the exercise of the voting rights is restricted under provisions limiting voting rights in the bylaws to a maximum of 26% or if the legal entity who ultimately may exercise the blocking minority does not change.

[166] A partial offer, aimed at the acquisition of a certain percentage of all equities or the acquisition of a certain class of equities of a target company, may only be structured as a purely voluntary offer (not aimed at obtaining control). In case of a partial offer, the principle of equal treatment set forth in section 3 of the Austrian Takeover Act must be observed. Therefore, it must be aimed either at all equity holders or at all holders of a particular class of equity.

3.6.3 Procedure

[167] The Austrian Takeover Act provides for a strictly regulated procedure that must be followed.

[168] The bidder is obliged to hire a suitably qualified expert (i.e., a sworn auditor and audit company which has contracted professional liability insurance, as well as certain credit institutions and financial institutions) to review and certify the bid documentation. Furthermore, the bidder must disclose without undue delay its intention to make a public offer and it must inform the administrative bodies of the target company of such an offer via press agencies and international news services (APA, Bloomberg, Reuters, etc.) once its administrative bodies have firmly decided to make an offer, or if circumstances oblige the bidder to make an offer (e.g., acquisition of control), or if substantial price movements or rumours/speculations regarding an upcoming offer occur.

[169] After the bidder makes its intention (to make a public offer) public, it must file the bid documentation as well as the report and the certificate of the expert with the Takeover Commission within ten trading days or within twenty trading days of acquiring a controlling interest. The offer documentation must contain the information specified by the Austrian Takeover Act, such as the content of the offer, information about the bidder, the consideration offered (and in case of a mandatory bid, the valuation method is applied) as well as the time limit for the acceptance of the offer.

[170] Between the twelfth and fifteenth trading day after the Austrian Takeover Commission has been notified, the bid documentation, together with the certificate of the expert, must be published either in a newspaper which is available nationwide in Austria or in the form of a brochure which is provided free of charge to the public by the target company at its registered office and by the (financial) institutions entrusted with the task of paying the consideration, except in case the Takeover Commission prohibits their publication.

3.6.4 Consideration

[171] Based on our experience, cash consideration is most common whereas offering shares (or combinations of both) is rather rare. However, sellers do not infrequently explore alternative ways such as the assumption of debt by a buyer, sometimes in combination with a cash payment.

[172] Mandatory offers always require cash consideration, but may have a paper alternative in addition thereto. The same applies to voluntary takeover offers aimed at obtaining control. Only purely voluntary offers (not aimed at obtaining control) may be in cash or securities. The price of a mandatory bid or a voluntary bid aimed at obtaining control may not be less than the highest consideration paid in cash or agreed on by the bidder (or by any entity acting in concert with the bidder) for the relevant equity security of the target company within the last twelve months prior to filing the offer. Furthermore, the price must at least correspond to the average stock exchange price of the respective equity security weighted by the respective trading volumes during the last six months prior to the day on which the intention to make an offer was announced. Further thresholds apply in case of a delisting offer and in case of certain measures relating to corporate law.

3.6.5 Conditions

[173] In general, mandatory offers may not be conditional on acceptance or any internal approvals by the bidder. It may solely be subject to obtaining regulatory clearance (e.g., merger control).

[174] Voluntary offers aimed at obtaining control are subject to a statutory acceptance threshold of more than 50% of the voting rights (which may be combined with a higher minimum acceptance threshold in the offer). Apart from that, the completion of purely voluntary offers (i.e., not aimed at obtaining control) and voluntary takeover offers aimed at obtaining control may be subject to objectively justified conditions, including minimum or maximum acceptance thresholds, clearance by merger control and other regulatory authorities or absence of an objectively determinable material adverse change. However, the fulfilment of a condition may not depend on the buyer's discretion. If conditions are unjustified, discretionary or not objectively determinable, an offer may be declared unlawful by the Takeover Commission. As a result, the latter may prohibit its launch. Therefore, it is advisable to consult the competent authority prior to submitting an offer, in particular as regards conditions which are unusual, may be held not precise enough or where their justification is not clearly evident.

[175] Furthermore, rights of withdrawal are permitted if they are objectively justified, in particular, if the exercising of the right of withdrawal does not depend exclusively on the discretion of the bidder.

3.6.6 Suspension of Voting Rights

[176] If the provisions of the Austrian Takeover Act are breached, the acquisition of shares remains valid. However, section 34 of the Austrian Takeover Act sets forth the suspension of voting rights. Moreover, section 35 of the Austrian Takeover Act stipulates penalties.

3.6.7 Timetable

[177] Public takeovers usually take a minimum of three and up to six months from the announcement of the offer to closing (hence, not including any time requirements for preparatory work). For larger international M&A transactions, including a competitive tender process and usual regulatory approval requirements, time periods may extend up to approximately twelve or even eighteen months from the first sell-side preparatory steps through to closing.

3.6.8 Squeeze-Out/Sell-Out

[178] The Austrian Minority Shareholders Squeeze-Out Act (*Gesellschafterausschlussgesetz*; *GesAusG*) allows a majority shareholder holding directly or indirectly at least 90% of the shares to squeeze out remaining minority shareholders. The consent of minority shareholders is not required, and therefore, such procedure may not be blocked by the respective shareholders. However, they are entitled to adequate cash compensation which is, on request, subject to a judicial review mechanism as to the adequate amount. Moreover, the articles of association may contain an exclusion of the squeeze-out right (opting out) or introduce a higher threshold.

[179] The Austrian Minority Shareholders Squeeze-Out Act provides for a specific procedure for such squeeze-out. In essence, a squeeze-out must be resolved by the shareholders' meeting based on a prior management report and supervisory board report, if any, which must set out in detail the cash compensation. This report must be audited by an independent certified public accountant appointed by the court. The cash compensation must be paid to the account of an escrow agent appointed by the majority shareholder. After a positive resolution on the squeeze-out and the registration of such resolution with the companies register, the shares of the minority shareholders automatically transfer to the majority shareholder against payment of the cash compensation. The cash compensation may subsequently be reviewed by a court, if minority shareholders object.

[180] A squeeze-out subsequent to a takeover bid is possible if the bid covered the acquisition of all shares and the shareholders' meeting approved the squeeze-out within three months after the expiration of the term of the bid. In case of a squeeze-out subsequent to a takeover bid, a majority shareholder is defined as a single shareholder (or a bidding consortium) which holds at least 90% of the total voting share capital and at least 90% of the voting rights. Such majority shareholder is entitled to demand the transfer of the voting shares of a minority shareholder. If the majority shareholder also holds 90% of the total share capital, the automatic transfer also includes shares without voting rights. The cash compensation paid within such a squeeze-out procedure may not be less than the highest consideration paid in the public offer. In case 90% of the shares were acquired under or in connection with the public offer, it is assumed that the compensation for the squeeze-out is adequate if it corresponds to the highest consideration paid in the public offer. The squeeze-out right under this special regime is mandatory and may not be excluded by amending the articles of association.

3.7 Other Relevant Selected Laws and Selected Due Diligence Issues

3.7.1 Anti-bribery/Anti-corruption Laws

[181] Under Austrian law, it is punishable to offer or grant a benefit for the execution or omission of a legal act by a member of the executive or supervisory board as well as an employee or representative of an undertaking, which is in breach of their duties. The same applies to demanding or accepting such benefits. Any benefit of a material or immaterial nature which is useful to the offender and to which he has no legal claim is regarded as a benefit.

[182] Any conduct that constitutes a violation of the law, a professional code, a contractual relationship (e.g., an employment contract) or an instruction applicable to the business activities of the respective person is considered to be in breach of duty.

[183] Austrian law provides for further criminal penalties in connection with (attempted) bribery of a public official.

[184] The aforementioned penalties are rigorously enforced by competent authorities and courts.

3.7.2 Money-Laundering Regulations

[185] The current anti-money laundering provisions are based on the 4th EU AML-Directive (*Directive (EU) 2015/849*), which has been implemented partly into the existing legal framework (e.g., for traders, gambling service providers, attorneys, notaries), and partly in separate laws (the Financial Markets Money Laundering Act (*Finanzmarkt-Geldwäschegesetz*; *FM-GwG*) for banks, credit and financial institutions and the Beneficial Owner Register Act (*Wirtschaftliche Eigentümer Registergesetz*; *WiEReG*) for the establishment of a register of beneficial owners). However, the European Parliament has already adopted the 5th EU AML-Directive (*Directive (EU) 2018/843*), which will lead to even more stringent requirements.

[186] Generally speaking, for certain risk-generating activities and transactions, such as opening a bank account to transfer a purchase price or execute a financial transaction, an AML/KYC check is required. The following, in particular, are required to carry out such an AML/KYC check: banks, notaries, trustees and members of consulting professions such as lawyers. In the course of such an AML/KYC check it is necessary to trace the beneficial owner of the respective entity and to provide the competent authority with the proper documentation, including group charts, register excerpts from intermediary companies (if any) as well as copies of identification documents of the beneficial owners. If no such beneficial owners can be determined, the competent authority must be provided with copies of identification documents of the managing directors of the respective entity. The process of determining an entity's beneficial owner(s) (if any) may be very arduous and time-consuming and it is therefore recommended to allow for enough time for such AML/KYC checks.

3.7.3 Environmental Considerations

[187] The federal parliament in Austria is empowered by the Austrian constitution to legislate and enact laws concerning business and industrial activity, water and hazardous waste and excessive emission levels. Worth mentioning is the fact that the federal provinces also have the competence to pass environmental legislation. Due to its EU-membership, Austria is obliged to implement EU environmental directives. In comparison to EU environmental provisions, Austria's environmental laws are, in many areas, stricter than required under EU legislation.

[188] Before starting to operate a plant in Austria, compliance with the provisions of the Austrian Trade Regulations (*Gewerbeordnung*; *GewO*) has to be ensured. The owner has to apply for a permit from the trade authority, which decides whether or not to grant an operating licence according to certain criteria:

- dangers to: water quality; life, health or property of employees and neighbours;
- pollution caused by smoke, noise and comparable emissions.

[189] There are numerous other public laws regulating environmental matters: That is, the consumption of water resources, industrial waste water discharges, etc. are subject to the Austrian Water Act. The Hazardous Waste Act regulates the distributor's obligation in relation to the treatment, storage and disposal of hazardous waste. The Austrian Chemical Act obliges producers of new chemicals to inform the Federal Ministry of Environment of their intention. In case of notification of dangerous chemicals, the Ministry may limit or prohibit their use. Several provincial laws, the Trade Regulations and the Ozone Act (which fixes the current emission level) deal with air pollution. Certain private and public projects (e.g., airports, power stations and other projects exceeding a specific size) need to submit an environmental impact statement to be authorized under the Environmental Impact Assessment Law. Additionally, the Criminal Code provides criminal penalties for environmental offences.

[190] Environmental provisions can also be found in the Civil Code, where, e.g., tort law and neighbour's property rights are regulated, which may impose liability on a party causing contamination. Therefore, even if a plant is operated in accordance with Austrian Public Law (i.e., under a valid operating licence, in accordance with Hazardous Waste Law, etc.), civil actions may still be brought forward against the owner of the plant under the Civil Code.

3.7.4 Intellectual Property Rights

Copyright

[191] The Austrian Copyright Act (*Urheberrechtsgesetz*; *UrhG*) provides protection for 'works' of an author, which are original intellectual creations in the field of literature, music, fine arts and cinematography. The individual original achievement must stand out from ordinary works. It is thus not sufficient for the work to be statistically unique. The creation must have a certain peculiarity, which is a result of the mental activity of its author. Neighbouring (or related) rights, ranging from performances, recitations, photographs (irrespective of whether they also qualify as works of fine art), audio recordings, broadcastings, databases (irrespective of whether they also qualify as collective works) and editions of posthumous work are also, although less extensively, protected.

[192] The copyright protection is granted as soon as the work is created; no formal requirements need to be fulfilled (e.g., a register entry). The author is the individual (the natural person) who created it.

[193] The Copyright Act protects the creator's economic and moral interests in the work. A number of exclusive exploitation and moral rights are provided for the:

- right of adaptation and translation;
- right of reproduction (right to copy the work by any means and to any extent);
- right of distribution (right to distribute copies of the work);
- right of rental;

- broadcasting right (right to broadcast the work);
- right of recitations, performance and presentation (right to publicly perform, recite or display the work);
- right of making the work available to the public (i.e., via Internet);
- right to claim authorship in the work;
- right to decide whether the author should be credited on the occasion of using the work;
- right to object to any distortion, mutilation or other modification of the work.

[194] Copyrights are inheritable but not transferable within the meaning of a full assignment. However, the author may grant an exploitation permit (non-exclusive licence) or an unlimited exploitation right (exclusive licence) to a third party, authorizing the use of the work in a specific manner. Some types of exploitation rights of certain works are administered by collecting societies (*Verwertungsgesellschaften*). The author may join a collecting society, which then grants permission to use the works under appropriate conditions and for an adequate consideration.

[195] Generally, the term of copyright for literature, musical and artistic works is seventy years following the death of the author (or the last surviving co-author). In case of cinematographic works, the protection expires seventy years after the last of the following person's death: i.e., main director; author of the script; author of the dialogues and author of the music. Neighbouring rights such as performances or photographs enjoy a uniform protection of fifty years and posthumous works twenty-five years after their edition.

[196] Civil law claims based on copyright infringements are subject to jurisdiction in trade matters. They are heard by the competent Regional Courts with local jurisdiction as commercial courts in first instance. Appeals have to be brought before the Regional Courts of Appeal and, in the final instance, before the Supreme Court. In civil proceedings, the author or an exclusive right holder may claim injunctive relief, removal of the source of infringement and the infringing products, rendering of accounts, adequate compensation (irrespective of fault), damages (in the event of fault), publication of the judgment and information of the source of supplier. Preliminary injunctions can also be granted to, *inter alia*, secure the cease-and-desist claim. Intentional infringements also constitute a criminal offence.

Trademarks

[197] Trademarks are defined by the Austrian Trademark Protection Act (*Markenschutzgesetz*; *MSchG*) as special signs used in the course of business and capable of distinguishing goods and services of one company from goods and services of another company. The sign must be represented in a manner, which enables the competent authority and the public to determine the clear and precise subject matter of the protection afforded to its proprietor. An Austrian trademark is filed with the Austrian Patent Office (*Österreichisches Patentamt*; *APO*). European trademarks (EUTM) are applied for and registered via the European Union Intellectual Property Office (EUIPO). They are valid in all Member States of the EU. The central authority under the intellectual property international system is the International Bureau of the World Intellectual Property Organization.

[198] In principle, trademarks are protected against confusingly similar signs, only if used for identical or similar products (likelihood of confusion). However, the scope of protection is extended for well-known trademarks: it protects such trademarks against a use without due cause, which takes unfair advantage of, or is detrimental to, the distinctive character or the repute of the earlier trademark. In this case, it is irrelevant whether the goods and services described by the sign are different from those, which the trademark is registered for.

[199] The following signs, for instance, cannot be registered. Signs that:

- consist only of coats of arms, flags or other state symbols, official signs and hallmarks, international organizations, etc.;
- lack distinctiveness;
- consist exclusively of signs or indications that have become customary in the current language or in the bona fide and established practices of the trade to designate the goods or services (i.e., generic words);
- contain representations or inscriptions that are scandalous or contrary to bonos mores; or
- are deceptive.

[200] Furthermore, descriptive signs, consisting exclusively of signs or indications, which may serve, in trade, to designate, e.g., the kind, quality, quantity, intended purpose of a product, may only be registered provided that the sign is considered by the public to be a distinctive representation of the goods and services of the applicant's business (secondary meaning).

[201] The application for registration has to specify the goods and services for which the mark is intended to be used. The application undergoes a formal examination and an examination of legality by the legal department of the APO. If an application is objected, the applicant has the right to submit written comments within a certain period of time. If objections raised by the APO cannot be dispelled, the application is dismissed. As of 1 September 2017, the automatically performed similarity search, which contains a list of identical trademarks or confusingly similar, already registered trademarks, is no longer obligatory when applying for a trademark. However, the applicant is still able to request an optional similarity research. Prior conflicting trademarks do not impede the registration of a trademark, but they can be invoked in opposition and/or cancellation proceedings. After the registration procedure is completed, the mark is registered in the trademark register and published.

[202] The registered trademark allows the owner to exclude others in the course of business to use:

- an identical sign for goods and services identical with those the trademark is registered for;
- an identical or similar sign for identical or similar goods and services if the likelihood of confusion (including the likelihood to associate the sign with the trade mark) is entailed.

[203] The protection of well-known trademarks is even broader (*see* above). The term of protection for trademarks is set at ten years, to be counted from the application date. The new regime fully applies to trademarks registered after 1 September 2018. For all trademarks registered prior to this date, there are transitional provisions.

[204] Civil law claims regarding trademark infringements fall under the exclusive jurisdiction of the Commercial Court of Vienna. The owner may claim injunctive relief (including a preliminary injunction), removal of the interference and the infringing products, accounting, payment of an adequate compensation, damages (in the event of fault), publication of the judgment, and information of the source of supplier. Intentional trademark infringement also constitutes a criminal offence.

Patents

[205] The Austrian Patent Act (*Patentgesetz*; *PatG*) provides for the protection of inventions, which are novel, inventive (not obvious to an expert) and capable of industrial application. The Austrian Patent Act excludes certain inventions from patentability, such as inventions being contrary to bonos mores; others are not regarded as inventions, for instance, scientific theories. The inventor or his legal successor has the right to be granted a patent. The first person applying for the patent is deemed to be the inventor, until the contrary is proven. An employee is generally entitled to the grant of a patent, unless otherwise provided by a written agreement (e.g., in the employment contract or in the form of a collective bargaining agreement). If such an agreement exists, the employee has to report any invention to the employer. In the latter case, an employee is entitled to special and fair remuneration.

[206] The application for a patent must be filed with the APO. It has to embody a full disclosure of the invention, so that a review by the examiner is possible. The application is refused, if formal defects are not removed and objections as to the patentability are not dispelled. The priority of a patent relates to the date of its application, which is published eighteen months after filing. Following this, third parties may object to the patentability. If there are no objections, the patent is granted, published in the Patent Gazette and a patent certificate is issued. Within four months of the date of the publication, one can oppose the granting of a patent. Due to the complex examination procedure, patent application proceedings sometimes extend over years.

[207] The maximum protection period of a patent is twenty years from the filing date onwards. The patent expires before the end of the twenty-year term if the annual fee is not paid or the patent owner waives his right to the patent. Granted patents may also be withdrawn, revoked or declared invalid under certain circumstances.

[208] The patent gives its owner an exclusive right to the commercial production and general use of the invention. A person having used the invention in bona fide within Austria prior to patenting may continue using the patent in his own business, since the granting of a patent does not affect the so-called pre-user.

[209] In case of a patent infringement, the owner has a claim for injunctive relief (including a preliminary injunction), removal of the channels of commerce/ destruction, rendering of accounts, publication of judgment, financial claims (adequate remuneration/damages), as well as information about the source of supplier. Intentional patent infringements constitute a criminal offence.

Further Intellectual Property Rights

[210] The Austrian law system further provides protection for models/designs (protected by the Design Protection Act (*Musterschutzgesetz*; *MSchuG*)) and utility models (protected by the Utility Model Act (*Gebrauchsmustergesetz*; *GebmG*)). Models are prototypes for the design of industrial products; utility models are technical developments, which do not have a high inventive level for protection under the Patent Act.

Verification for Due Diligence Purposes

[211] The Austrian Patent Office provides an online information portal, which allows for searches for trademarks, designs, patents and utility models (SEE.IP). Additionally, the eSearch plus application by the EUIPO enables searches for EUTM and Registered Community Designs within EUIPO's databases.

3.7.5 Agents

[212] The Commercial Agents Act (*Handelsvertretergesetz*; *HVertrG*) defines an agent as a person who is permanently appointed by an entrepreneur (the principal) with the negotiation or conclusion of business transactions (except on immovable property) in his name and on his behalf and who carries out such activity independently and commercially.

[213] Pursuant to section 24 of the Commercial Agents Act, the agent is entitled to an appropriate compensation after the agency contract has terminated if and to the extent that:

- he has provided the principal with new customers or significantly expanded existing business relationships;
- it may be expected that the principal continues to derive considerable benefits from such business relationships after the termination of the agency contract; and
- the payment of such compensation is equitable, taking into account all circumstances, in particular, the commissions lost by the agent on the business transacted with the respective customers.

[214] The compensation shall not exceed an annual remuneration calculated on the basis of the average of the last five years. If the agency contract has lasted less than five years, the compensation shall be calculated on the basis of the average of the entire contractual period.

[215] The agent shall have no claim for compensation if:

- the agent has (prematurely) terminated the agency contract, unless circumstances attributable to the principal have given rise to such termination or the agent cannot reasonably be expected to continue his activity due to his age or sickness; or
- the principal has (prematurely) terminated the agency contract due to certain culpable conduct of the agent; or
- the agent assigns rights and obligations under the agency contract to a third party.

[216] Furthermore, the agent shall lose the right to compensation if he has not notified the principal within one year of termination of the agency contract that he intends to exercise his above-mentioned rights.

3.7.6 Change of Control Clauses

[217] Change of control clauses are commonly found in contracts where the identity of the contracting party and the shareholders standing behind such contracting party are of importance to the respective other party. Frequent examples are banking loan or other financing agreements with banks, subsidy/grant agreements, license, leasing or rental agreements, long-term (or frame) supply, customer, distribution and agency agreements, as well as shareholder agreements. Along the legal consequences of such a clause, one may distinguish two types of change of control clauses: Those giving a party the right to terminate the contract or alter its terms in a specific way, and those where a change of control automatically triggers termination of the contract or alteration of its terms in a specific way. Either of these types is usually enforceable. Please note that apart from the world of contracts, also public licenses and permits/authorization may be based on a certain shareholder/owner structure and may therefore be affected in case of a change of control (or even without actually changing control where the shareholder structure changes), triggering possible termination or revocation of such licenses/permits/authorizations. This holds particularly true for permits in certain industry sectors, such as the banking, finance and insurance industry, where fit and proper tests of the given shareholder(s) are an essential prerequisite for granting and upholding the respective business license.

3.8 The Due Diligence Process

[218] The due diligence practice developed in Anglo-American countries has also been well-established and adopted in Austria for quite some time now and is a standard part of any fairly substantial M&A or financing transaction, whether international or national. Therefore, an Austrian due diligence process, the way it is set up and conducted (the use of – now predominantly virtual – data rooms, non-disclosure agreements, etc.), the focus on red flags and key issues, the recommendations for contractual safeguarding in light of the outcomes of the due diligence (usually certain reps and warranties or indemnities or conditions precedent or price reduction, or adaptation of the acquisition structure, as appropriate), will hold few surprises for those with experience in such matters.

[219] Parties of an M&A transaction rely on the statutory warranty regime only in extremely rare cases (and in fact, the Austrian statutory warranty regime is not suitable for the complexities and different settings of companies in M&A transactions), but rather includes their own warranty regime into the respective agreement. Such warranties set forth in the agreement are usually based on, and drafted in accordance with, the results of a due diligence carried out beforehand. The results of a due diligence process may also warrant the inclusion of indemnities (against known risks), or certain conditions precedents, or certain carve-outs or other structural changes in the M&A contract. Contract drafting considerations, deriving from the outcomes of a due diligence process, would typically also be applied in relation to contractually stipulated rules and regulations on the legal consequences in case of a breach of warranties, including the type of remedies, scope or recovery and respective limitations. The warranties, indemnities, conditions precedent requested as a consequence of the due diligence results, and the remedies and limitations to remedies often become a core part of negotiations among the parties of the contractual documentation.

[220] The determination of the scope of the due diligence to be carried out is usually decision-based primarily on the director's duty to act foremost in the best interest of the company and in accordance with the business judgment rule (*see* 3.5.2), knowledge of the relevant market and the target itself as well as its area of business. Furthermore, the size, complexity and significance of the transaction (in particular, the transaction volume, the complexity of the transaction or the target, and the risk potentials typically suspected in targets of such type) play an important role when defining the scope of the due diligence.

[221] An example of a peculiarity of an Austrian due diligence process can be seen in the lawyers' typical attempt to establish a chain of title to shares in a company back to its initial establishment/incorporation. This is relevant insofar as pursuant to Austrian law, all subsequent share transfers would be void, in case one of the previous buyers did not acquire title to the respective shares, and the possibility to acquire shares in a company by a bona fide purchaser from a non-owner is practically close to zero since it is almost impossible to establish a chain of title with absolute certainty, a 'plausibility check' is typically carried out. In the course of such plausibility check, registers are usually consulted (i.e., the Commercial Register in case of limited liability companies, or the share ledger of a company in case of a private stock corporation having issued registered shares) in which the history of the shareholdings has been (or should have been if done correctly) registered. However, such registrations are only of declaratory nature and thus only of some indicative, but not conclusive, evidence of the share title chain. In addition, lawyers would therefore request the contractual documents showing how the title to the respective shares has passed from the original shareholder to the current seller.

3.9 Dispute Resolution

[222] In principle, the Austrian judicial system knows up to three instances. There are 115 District Courts (*Bezirksgerichte*), 20 Provincial Courts (*Landesgerichte*), four Circuit Courts of Appeals (*Oberlandesgerichte*) and the Supreme Court (*Oberste Gerichtshof*; *OGH*) in Austria. Furthermore, the court structure in Austria is characterized by a division into courts of ordinary jurisdiction (criminal and civil law courts) and public law courts (constitutional and administrative law). The primary characteristics of all Austrian courts are that the judges are *ex lege* irremovable, independent in their decision-making and do not follow any instructions issued by other institutions.

[223] If a party from a foreign country is involved in a dispute in front of an Austrian court, they will be treated in the same way as a local party. However, it should be noted that foreign claimants without sufficient funds in Austria can be imposed a security for legal costs if the court decision is not enforceable at the place of residence of the claimant. Also, it may take longer for hearings to take place because the judges take equal account of the availability of both parties as it is, e.g., easier and quicker to come to Austria for a hearing from another country within Europe than from other continents. Under certain conditions, testimonies and witness statements may be delivered via video conference, even though some judges prefer to hear parties and witnesses personally in the courtroom. Additional costs may arise for the translation of documents, as Austrian courts usually do not accept foreign language evidence (even if in English). The same applies to court hearings in Austria. The court hearings are therefore conducted in German. For witnesses and parties who do not speak German as a mother tongue, an interpreter must be appointed, which also incurs additional costs (like other costs, e.g., court fees, attorney fees, expert costs, etc., these are to be borne by the losing party, either in total or on a pro rata basis, as the case may be). The average time between the filing of a claim and the first hearing is usually not more than two or three months. It should be noted that the first hearing usually only serves the purpose of settlement talks (where possible) and to establish the future timetable of the proceedings. Usually, the taking of evidence and, in particular, the hearing of witnesses takes place in subsequent hearings.

[224] It can become more complicated and time-consuming where not only a foreign party is involved but also foreign law is to be applied by an Austrian court, i.e., on the basis of a contractual agreement. In those cases, it can be quite a 'balancing act' between the legal obligation of the court to inform itself about the applicable provisions of the applicable foreign law and the interest of the plaintiff to prepare and 'present' these provisions to the court. Although the court is obliged to form its own view of the applicable law ex officio, the applicable rules of Austrian conflict law permit it to decide on the basis of Austrian law, if the applicable foreign law cannot be assessed within a reasonable time. The party intending to invoke a foreign provision to its advantage should, therefore, in its own interest, offer the necessary (legal) information to the court.

[225] All key contractual provisions, if they have a legal basis in applicable law and are not, in particular, against good morals, are enforceable in front of the national courts. A few years ago, the Austrian Unfair Competition Act (*Gesetz gegen den unlauteren Wettbewerb*; *UWG*) implemented new rules to safeguard business secrets in litigation, thus reducing a possible impediment to the enforcement of claims. However, procedures can take quite a long time until they result in an enforceable title. This particularly holds true for shareholder disputes and warranty disputes, e.g., in construction litigation, where the duration of the proceedings in first instance lasting for several years is not uncommon. Depending on the amount in dispute and the legal questions raised, there can be up to three instances of courts deciding on a matter. Under certain circumstances, hearings or instances of taking of evidence may need to be repeated or completed in the course of a litigation. Obtaining expert opinions can also considerably extend the duration of proceedings and increase the costs involved significantly. All in all, a decision can hardly be expected at first instance within the first year of litigation, in particular, more complex cases can take several years in first instance. Exceptions to this are, of course, preliminary injunctions, where decisions are made much more quickly – if necessary, also on short notice and within a few days. Also, ex parte decisions are possible in urgent cases; however, the opposite party is granted advanced legal remedies in case it was not heard in first instance. Again, the court may impose securities on the applicant to be paid before the preliminary injunction becomes enforceable.

4 MERGER CONTROL, ANTITRUST AND COMPETITION ISSUES

4.1 General

[226] The main sources of provisions on antitrust and merger control are the Austrian Cartel Act (*Kartellgesetz 2005*; *KartG*) and the Austrian Competition Act (*Wettbewerbsgesetz*; *WettbG*). The Cartel Act not only governs horizontal cartels but also contains provisions on vertical agreements, non-binding recommendations by associations, merger control and abuse of a dominant position. The Austrian Cartel Act and Competition Act have been amended as of 10 September 2021 (*KaWeRÄG 2021*). The main purpose of the amendment was the implementation of the ECN+ Directive. However, the Austrian legislator used the opportunity to modernize the Austrian Cartel Act by, *inter alia*, introducing a second domestic turnover threshold and the SIEC test for merger control, and by strengthening companies' ability to engage in sustainability cooperations.

4.2 Merger Control

[227] The European Merger Control Regulation (Council Regulation (EEC) No. 139/2004) is directly applicable in Austria. According to Article 21 of the Merger

Control Regulation, Austrian law will generally not apply in case of a merger having a community dimension. However, if such merger constitutes or strengthens or is likely to constitute or strengthen the undertaking's dominant position in the Austrian relevant market, the Commission may refer the case to the National Competition Authority in Austria under Article 9 of the Merger Control Regulation. In addition, media concentrations fulfilling the Austrian thresholds must be notified in Austria, even if the concentration has a community dimension and the Merger Control Regulation applies.

[228] If a concentration does not reach a community dimension, and therefore, the Merger Control Regulation is not applicable, concentrations within the meaning of the Cartel Act have to be notified to the Federal Competition Authority before implementation, if certain requirements are fulfilled (*see* paragraphs [230] to [232] below). Pursuant to section 7 Cartel Act, the following transactions result in a concentration:

- the acquisition of an undertaking, as a whole or of a substantial part of it, by an undertaking, especially by way of merger or conversion;
- the acquisition by an undertaking of rights in the business of another undertaking by means of operational lease or management agreements;
- the direct or indirect acquisition of shares in an undertaking by another undertaking if, as a result, the participation held after the acquisition is or exceeds 25%, or is or exceeds 50%;
- as a result, at least half of the management or members of the supervisory boards of two or more undertakings are identical;
- any other connection of undertakings which allows one undertaking to have a direct or indirect dominant influence over another undertaking.

[229] Certain full-function joint ventures are also deemed concentrations under the Cartel Act.

[230] Concentrations meeting the following thresholds (they refer to the last business year preceding the transaction) will have to be notified prior to implementation (pre-merger notification):

- combined worldwide turnover of EUR300 m (in case of media companies and media services, their turnover should be multiplied by a factor of 200, of media support companies by a factor of 20 to meet this threshold);
- combined turnover in Austria of EUR30 m, of which the annual Austrian turnover of at least two of the undertakings concerned is greater than EUR1 million each; (in case of media companies and media services their turnover should be multiplied by a factor of 200, of media support companies by a factor of 20 to meet these thresholds); and
- at least two undertakings concerned have a worldwide turnover of EUR5 m each.

[231] However, concentrations exceeding these turnover thresholds are exempt from mandatory notification if only one undertaking achieved a turnover in Austria of more than EUR5 m and the other undertaking(s) achieved an aggregate turnover of not more than EUR30 m worldwide (in case of media companies and media services their turnover should be multiplied by a factor of 200, of media support companies by a factor of 20 to meet this worldwide threshold).

[232] Furthermore, an additional threshold is applicable under Austrian merger control law as of 1 November 2017, which is linked not only to the turnover of the undertakings involved but also to the transaction value. Specifically, concentrations not meeting the above-mentioned but the following thresholds must be notified to the Federal Competition Authority:

- combined worldwide turnover of more than EUR300 m;
- combined turnover in Austria of more than EUR15 m;
- where the value of the consideration exceeds EUR200 m; and
- if the target company has significant business operations in Austria.

[233] A notification of a concentration must contain detailed information about the undertakings concerned, as well as general information on the market structure, in order to enable the Cartel Court to decide whether or not the concentration creates or strengthens a dominant position in the relevant market. In addition, since the beginning of 2022, the 'SIEC' test ('Significant Impediment to Effective Competition'), which is the test used in EU merger control to examine mergers for their compatibility with a competitive market, is also applied in Austrian competition law (section 12(1)(2) Cartel Act). However, the wording chosen by the Austrian legislator deviates from that of Article 2 (2) and (3) of the European Merger Control Regulation in that market dominance is not set out as a standard example of a significant impediment to effective competition, but is placed alongside it as an equivalent case of application. After notification, the Federal Competition Authority publishes the core facts of the concentration on its homepage.

[234] Within four weeks upon the receipt of the notification, the Federal Competition Authority and the Federal Cartel Prosecutor (the 'Official Parties') conduct an initial assessment ('Phase I') and, most commonly, following the lapse of this four-week period (which may be prolonged to a maximum of six weeks), the transaction is deemed cleared. In more critical cases, the Federal Competition Authority or the Federal Cartel Prosecutor initiates the main examination proceedings ('Phase II'). In such a case, the Cartel Court has five months to finalize the investigations, assess whether the transaction creates or strengthens a dominant market position, or significantly impedes effective competition (*see* paragraph [233] above) and, finally, either to issue a clearance decision (which may be subject to conditions and/or obligations) or to prohibit the concentration (which is quite rare in practice).

Importantly, the Cartel Court can approve mergers despite the existence of grounds for prohibition (section 12(2) Cartel Act). In particular, (i) if it is to be expected that the merger will also lead to improvements in the conditions of competition which outweigh the disadvantages of the merger; (ii) the concentration is necessary to maintain or improve the international competitiveness of the undertakings concerned and is economically justified; or (iii) the economic advantages substantially outweigh the disadvantages of the merger.

Appeals against decisions of the Cartel Court have to be filed with the Supreme Court within four weeks.

[235] The Cartel Act provides that third parties affected by the concentration have the right to file comments within fourteen days from publication of the notification (in Phase I). In the course of Phase II proceedings, third parties are entitled to submit written comments to the Cartel Court at any time. However, they do not acquire party status, do not have any procedural rights, and cannot challenge a clearance decision.

[236] In case a concentration has been implemented without prior clearance ('gun-jumping'), the Cartel Court may impose a fine of up to 10% of the company's worldwide total revenue. Furthermore, contracts forming the basis of such transactions are, by law, deemed null and void.

4.3 Anti-competitive Restraints

4.3.1 Cartels

[237] Section 1 paragraph 1 of the Cartel Act determines that all agreements between undertakings, decisions by associations of undertakings and concerted practices, which have the prevention, restriction or distortion of competition as their object or effect, shall be prohibited. This essentially mirrors Article 101 paragraph 1 TFEU (*Treaty on the Functioning of the European Union*). Section 2 paragraph 1 of the Cartel Act is the equivalent to Article 101 paragraph 3 TFEU and lists justification requirements. Since the last amendment to the Cartel Act (*KaWeRÄG 2021*), there has been a newly inserted passage intended to enable cooperations between undertakings for the purpose of ecological sustainability by exempting agreements whose ecological benefits outweigh any disadvantages for the competition from the ban on cartels. Importantly, a direct consumer benefit is explicitly not required. There is an assumption of sufficient consumer participation if the benefit (efficiency gains) arising from the cooperation significantly contributes to an ecologically sustainable or climate-neutral economy.

[238] Section 1 of the Cartel Act and Article 101 TFEU are, in parallel, applicable, if the examined behaviour has an effect on the 'trade between Member States'; only in (rare) cases, where, for instance, only a regional market is affected, only national law (here: section 1 of the Cartel Act) applies.

[239] Restrictions 'by object' (so-called hard core restrictions) are, for instance, price fixing or market sharing between competitors or resale price maintenance between supplier and retailer. Such hard-core restrictions violate the cartel prohibition irrespective of the market position of the parties. For certain restrictions 'by effect', section 2 paragraph 2 of the Cartel Act foresees a '*de minimis*'-exemption, if the combined market share of competitors does not exceed 10% or if the market share held by each of the parties not competing with each other does not exceed 15% on the relevant markets.

[240] The Cartel Court may, upon application by an Official Party, impose substantial fines of up to 10% of the company's worldwide total revenue. Also, as under

EU law, agreements violating the cartel prohibition are by law null and void. Furthermore, damage claims based on competition law violations play an increasing role.

4.3.2 Abuse of a Dominant Position

[241] According to the Cartel Act, an undertaking is deemed to be dominant if it is neither exposed to any (considerable) competition on the relevant market, or if it has a paramount market position in relation to its competitors (due to, e.g., its financial power, its relations to other undertakings, its opportunities to access supply and sales markets, the significance of its intermediary services for other undertakings' access to supply and sales markets, its access to competition-relevant data, the benefits derived from network effects and other circumstances that restrict market entry for other undertakings etc.). Typically, an undertaking is deemed dominant and has to rebut this assumption (i) if its market shares exceed 30%, or (ii) if it has a market share of more than 5% and is exposed to competition by not more than two undertakings, (iii) or it has a market share of more than 5% and is one of the four biggest undertakings on this market, which together have a market share of at least 80%, (iv) or is part of a number of undertakings as suppliers or purchasers on the relevant market having a market share of more than 50% and consisting of three or fewer undertakings, or having a market share of at least two-thirds and consisting of five or fewer undertakings.

Moreover, pursuant to section 4a Cartel Act, an undertaking is also deemed to be dominant (relative market power), if it has a predominant market position in relation to its purchasers and suppliers; such a position exists in particular if the latter are dependent on the maintenance of the business relationship in order to avoid serious economic disadvantages. An undertaking which is active as an intermediary on a multi-sided digital market shall also be deemed to have a dominant market position if the customers of his intermediary services are dependent on the establishment of a business relationship in order to avoid serious economic disadvantages.

[242] As under EU law (Article 102 TFEU), the abuse of a dominant position is prohibited. Section 5 of the Cartel Act contains a non-exhaustive list of practices which may constitute an abuse, such as direct/indirect imposition of unreasonable purchase/selling prices, discrimination of business partners by imposing different conditions on similar transactions.

[243] The Cartel Court may, as the main sanction, impose substantial fines of up to 10% of the company's worldwide total revenue.

4.3.3 Anti-competitive Restraints after Closing

[244] Merger control clearances also cover ancillary restraints, to the extent that they are directly related to, and necessary for, the implementation of the transaction.

[245] No separate notification is required (or indeed possible) for agreements containing post-transaction restrictions. The European Commission's Ancillary Restraints Notice serves as a basis for Austrian courts to assess which types of restraints may be considered ancillary and thus covered by the clearance.

[246] In short, according to the principles of the Ancillary Restraints Notice, for instance, non-compete clauses (hindering the seller to be active post-transaction) are only of 'ancillary nature', if limitations apply regarding:

- duration (maximum of two to three years);
- geographic scope (region covered by target activities pre-transaction); and
- product scope (products supplied by the target pre-transaction).

[247] Non-solicitation and confidentiality clauses have a comparable effect and are therefore evaluated in a similar way to non-competition clauses.

5 TAXATION ASPECTS

5.1 Tax Authorities

[248] Taxes in Austria are levied by either the federal tax authorities (in case of federal taxes) or (in case of state and municipal taxes) by the municipalities. Besides the municipalities, since 1 January 2021, there are only two tax offices in Austria competent for taxes: The 'tax office Austria' (*Finanzamt Österreich*) and the 'tax office for large businesses' (*Finanzamt für Großbetriebe*), which is competent for businesses with a turnover of more than EUR10 m. Besides that, there is one customs office for Austria (*Zollamt Österreich*) and one authority competent for tax fraud, fiscal criminal law and fiscal police (*Amt für Betrugsbekämpfung*; *ABB*).

[249] The most important taxes like the corporate income tax, the value added tax (VAT), wage-related taxes, real estate transfer tax and duties are levied by the tax office Austria. The 'tax office for large businesses' is competent only for selected important taxes (like the corporate income tax and the VAT) of large businesses.

[250] All tax offices are subordinated to the Federal Minister of Finance who can advise the tax offices on how to deal with cases and also issues guidelines. Some matters, like unilateral tax relief, are directly handled by him or her.

[251] It is possible to appeal against assessments and other decisions to the Federal Fiscal Court or (in case of state and municipal taxes sometimes) other administrative courts. Decisions of the administrative courts can be appealed to the Supreme Constitutional and the Supreme Administrative Court, which are the highest instances in tax matters.

5.2 Important Taxes

5.2.1 Corporate Income Tax (*Körperschaftsteuer*)

[252] Corporations are subject to Corporate Income Tax in Austria. If the corporate entity's seat or place of effective management is located within Austria, it is subject to unlimited tax liability. In this case, corporations are subject to tax on their worldwide income.

[253] Other corporations are subject to limited tax liability only, which encompasses three cases:

(1) foreign corporations which have neither their place of management nor their seat in Austria are subject to tax only with domestic income;
(2) public bodies (like the federation, the states, municipalities, certain public associations and political parties) are subject to tax with certain income on which withholding tax is imposed or on which withholding tax would be imposed if it was domestic income;
(3) tax-exempt corporations are also subject to tax only with income on which withholding tax is imposed or on which withholding tax would be imposed if it was domestic income.

[254] The total taxable income is taxed at a flat rate of 25% until 2022. By 2023, the corporate income tax rate is 24%, and from 2024 onwards, the rate is 23%. There is a minimum corporate income tax (*Mindestkörperschaftssteuer*) for corporations with no or low taxable income. The minimum corporate income tax amounts to 5% of the minimum share capital of the entity per calendar year. A limited liability company would therefore have to pay EUR1 750 and a stock corporation EUR3 500 per year of minimum corporate tax. The paid minimum corporate tax is dealt as an advance payment for further corporate income tax.

[255] Foreign corporations do not pay a minimum tax. They are taxed either by an annual assessment or by way of deduction at source.

[256] Austrian tax law classifies all income received by a company as business income. No special rates apply to capital gains or losses. However, there are the following important exemptions.

National Participation Exemption (Nationale Schachtelbefreiung)

[257] Dividends paid from an Austrian corporation to another Austrian corporation are tax exempt regardless of the amount of participation or the holding period.

International Qualified Participation Exemption (Internationale Schachtelbefreiung)

[258] Dividends and capitals gains derived from participations in foreign corporations are tax exempt if the participation amounts to at least 10% and the shares are held for at least one year (subject to anti-abuse rules and CFC rules regarding attribution of foreign income to its domestic parent company).

International Portfolio Participation Exemption (Befreiung für Portfoliodividenden)

[259] Dividends from international participation below 10% are also tax exempt in most cases (subject to anti-abuse rules).

5.2.2 Income Tax (*Einkommensteuer*)

[260] Individuals are subject to Income Tax in Austria. Any person resident in Austria (i.e., any person whose domicile or customary place of abode is in Austria) is subject to unlimited tax liability, whereas non-residents are only subject to a limited tax liability (i.e., only on certain categories of income from Austrian sources). If an individual stays in the country for more than six months during a year, he is regarded as a resident.

[261] Seven categories of income exist in Austria:

(1) Income from agricultural and forestry activities.
(2) Income from professional or self-employed activities.
(3) Income from conducting a business.
(4) Income from dependent employment.
(5) Capital income.
(6) Income from rent and lease.
(7) Other income according to the Income Tax Act (*Einkommensteuergesetz*; *EStG*) (including certain recurring income, gains on speculative transactions).

[262] Donations, gifts, private lottery winnings and any other income which does not fall under one of those specific categories mentioned above is not taxable.

[263] The taxable income of resident taxpayers is taxed at the following graduated marginal rates between 0% and 55% (progressive rate) (applicable from 1 July 2022) (from 1 July 2023, the rate of 42% is reduced to 40%):

EUR1–EUR11 000	00%
EUR11 000–EUR18 000	20%
EUR18 000–EUR31 000	30%
EUR31 000–EUR60 000	42%
EUR60 000–EUR90 000	48%

EUR90 000–EUR1 000 000	50%
above EUR1 000 000	55%

Source: The tax rates and amounts are set forth in section 33 para. 1 of the Income Tax Act.

[264] The standard Austrian income tax rates are also applied to the income of non-resident individuals, with certain modifications and exceptions. Income of non-resident individuals is sometimes taxed by means of a flat withholding tax at source, which may also have the effect of a final all-in taxation.

[265] Double taxation relief in the form of a credit of foreign taxes or a reduction of or exemption from Austrian taxes may be granted under the applicable double tax treaty.

5.2.3 Value Added Tax (*Umsatzsteuer*)

[266] Austria has implemented the European VAT Directive 2006/112/EC on the common system of VAT.

[267] Therefore, the supply of goods and services by a taxable person for consideration is subject to VAT in Austria, if the place of supply is in Austria. Furthermore, the import of goods from a Non-EU Member State is subject to import VAT.

[268] The common VAT rate currently amounts to 20%; certain transactions are subject to a reduced rate of 10%. A tax rate of 13% applies to the supply of live animals, animal feed, plants, art objects, rental for residential purposes, revenues from artistic activities and operation of theatres, nature parks and swimming baths.

[269] Regardless of the legal form, any individual or corporation that carries on a business or professional activity producing revenues is a taxable person under the VAT Act (*Umsatzsteuergesetz*; *UStG*).

[270] It is possible to form VAT tax groups (*umsatzsteuerliche Organschaft*), which means that two or more corporations are treated as one taxpayer for VAT purposes and supplies between these entities are not taxable.

5.2.4 Taxes on the Transfer of Real Estate

[271] If Austrian real estate is transferred, real estate transfer tax (*Grunderwerbssteuer*) is payable at a rate of 3.5% of the higher (i) the purchase price for the real estate or (ii) the land value (*Grundstückswert)* of the real estate. In addition to the real estate transfer tax, a registration duty for the land register at a rate of 1.1% is charged if the purchaser is entered as the owner of the real estate in the Austrian land register.

[272] In certain cases, a lower rate of real estate transfer tax applies. According to section 7 paragraph 1 No. 2 lit c of the Austrian Real Estate Transfer Tax Act (*Grunderwerbsteuergesetz*; *GrEStG*), the real estate transfer tax for transfers of real estate in connection with a reorganization under the Reorganisation Tax Act (*Umgründungssteuergesetz*; *UmgrStG*) will, in general, amount to only 0.5% of the land value of the real estate. The 'land value' usually corresponds to 80%–100% of the fair market value. It is, in any case, not higher than the fair market value. It is assessed pursuant to the methods set forth in a regulation of the Ministry of Finance and it is also possible to prove the fair market value by an expert opinion. The 0.5% tax rate is a flat rate irrespective of the value. In addition, a registration duty for the land register at a rate of 1.1%, based on three times the even lower 'standard tax value' (*Einheitswert*) (limited to 30% of the fair market value), is levied.

[273] Real estate transfer tax also falls due if one person acquires 95% of the shares of a corporation that owns Austrian real estate. In this case, the tax also amounts to 0.5% of the land value (*see* above) of the real estate. No registration fee in the land register is due in this case.

[274] Furthermore, real estate transfer tax is triggered if Austrian real estate belongs to a partnership and within five years, 95% of the partners of the partnership change. The tax amounts to 0.5% of the tax value of the real estate is owed by the partnership.

5.2.5 Capital Duty

[275] The capital duty, which was levied on contributions to Austrian corporations, was abolished on 1 January 2016.

5.2.6 Stamp Duty

[276] Austria levies a stamp duty on certain kinds of legal transactions if a written deed is executed and a certain nexus to Austria exists. The following legal transactions are, *inter alia*, subject to a stamp duty, if these conditions are met:

Assignments of rights and receivables	0.8% of the consideration
Lease agreements (except residential lease)	1% of the contract value
Sureties	1% of the liability
Mortgages	1% of the liability
Out–of-court settlement agreements	1%–2% of the consideration

Source: The information included in the table is taken from the Austrian Stamp Duty Act.

[277] The stamp duty for credit and loan agreements was abolished in 2011. There are also important exemptions like for sureties and mortgages which secure obligations of borrowers under loan and credit agreements.

[278] The stamp duty can be legally avoided if no written deed is executed or no nexus to Austria exists (e.g., all documents are executed outside of Austria and all originals and certified copies remain outside of Austria and no 'substitute documentation' is produced in Austria or sent to or from Austria).

5.3 Tax Consolidation

[279] An Austrian resident corporation may form a tax group with domestic and foreign subsidiaries. The minimum period for a tax group is three years. The group parent must hold a direct and/or indirect participation of more than 50% of the share capital and voting rights of the respective subsidiary. Such participation must exist throughout the entire fiscal year of the respective tax group member. The participating companies must have the same balance sheet date.

[280] The parent company of a tax group (*Gruppenträger*) has to be a corporation either with its statutory seat and/or place of management in Austria (resident corporation) or an EU company with a domestic branch to which the participations belong. Domestic and foreign corporations domiciled in the EU and countries with mutual administrative assistance are eligible as group members (*Gruppenmitglieder*), although the latter only if they are first-tier foreign subsidiaries. Non-resident companies must be legally comparable to an Austrian corporation and must have their seat in another Member State or a state with which Austria has agreed to the comprehensive exchange of information. If and what type of income the group companies earn and if it is active or passive is irrelevant.

[281] For the formation of a tax group, a group taxation application must be filed before the end of that fiscal year for which the group companies' profits are to be pooled for the first time. Such application must be executed by the management boards of all Austrian corporations that wish to participate in the group. The tax authorities will then render a binding decision on whether the prerequisites necessary for establishing a tax group have been fulfilled.

[282] A tax allotment agreement (*Steuerumlagevereinbarung*) must be concluded between the affiliated corporations regarding the compensation of group members for corporate income taxes paid or not paid by the group parent as a result of the tax group (due to mandatory Austrian capital maintenance rules prohibiting the transfer of benefits from a corporation to its shareholder which are not in the form of declared dividends). Such compensatory payments (*Steuerumlagen*) are deemed to be tax neutral.

[283] Under the conditions mentioned above, the income and special allowances of the controlled group members are attributed to the income and reported in the tax return of the controlling parent company. As a result, corporate income tax is assessed at the level of the head of the tax group only. However, as this consolidation applies only for tax purposes, dividend distributions by a group member to an upper-tier group member/head of the tax group are feasible under the provisions of corporate law, as well.

[284] Foreign losses of the foreign corporations eligible as group members, which are calculated under domestic tax rules (at the maximum, the foreign loss calculated under foreign tax rules), are attributed proportionally to the upper-tier tax group member and subsequently to the head of the tax group.

[285] Generally, losses (of a group parent or a group member) can be deducted by the group parent only up to the amount of 75% of the profit of the respective year.

[286] If foreign tax losses are or could be set off abroad, the foreign loss is recaptured in Austria. A recapture also applies for any loss that was attributed to the tax group member/head of the tax group in the past without being recaptured afterwards, if the foreign corporation leaves the tax group. This applies analogously if the non-resident group member's economic situation is no longer comparable to its status when the losses were offset against Austrian profits. In the case of insolvency or liquidation of the foreign corporation, the recapture is limited so that the true and final loss of substance remains deductible.

[287] In the case of consolidated group taxation, interest and financing costs in connection with the acquisition of the controlled subsidiary corporation may be deducted from the tax base of the controlling parent corporation. Write-offs of participation are not deductible.

[288] The tax group is terminated if the group parent is merged, as this function is not transferable to another entity.

5.4 Tax Considerations Arising on M&A Transactions

5.4.1 Transfer of Shares

Share for Share Exchanges (Contributions of Shares)

[289] Article III of the Reorganisation Tax Act deals with the transfer of specified assets and provides for tax exemptions at the level of the transferor and the acquiring company, as well as at the level of the shareholders of the latter.

[290] The Reorganisation Tax Act is applicable to contributions of shares into a corporation if the contributed shares account for 25% of the target company. The Reorganisation Tax Act is also applicable if the shares transferred by several people amount together to more than 50% of the voting rights of the target company or if the shares result in more than 50% of the voting rights of the target company together with existing shares that the receiving company has in the target company. If the receiving company already holds 50% or more of the voting rights of the target company, the contribution of additional shares of the target company to the receiving company will also fall under the provisions of the Reorganisation Tax Act.

[291] As a general rule, the contribution of such qualifying shares is covered by the Reorganisation Tax Act if the transferor obtains only shares in the acquiring company as consideration. However, there are some exceptions where it is not necessary for the receiving company to issue shares. The most important case is the transfer of assets to wholly owned subsidiaries or indirect subsidiaries.

Acquiring Company

[292] If the contribution of shares falls under the Reorganisation Tax Act, the acquiring company usually has to continue the book values of the transferred shares. If the contributed shares were not subject to tax in Austria before the contribution, the receiving entity may account for the fair market value of the shares for tax purposes (step-up).

[293] Contributions of shares are generally not subject to VAT or other indirect taxes except for real estate transfer tax if more than 95% of the shares in a company holding Austrian real estate are transferred or united in the acquiring company (*see* 5.2.4).

Target Company

[294] The exchange of shares generally has no immediate impact on the acquired target company.

[295] If the new shareholder does not qualify for dividend withholding tax exemption (e.g., due to anti-abuse rules), the acquired company may have to withhold taxes from dividends to the new shareholder. However, under the Reorganisation Tax Act, the new shareholder will continue the holding period of the previous shareholder.

[296] Under basic principles of corporate income tax law, the deduction of losses is excluded in the case of the acquisition of a corporate shell (*Mantelkauf*). The rationale is that the company wishing to utilize the loss carry-forward does not only need to be legally identical (or the legal successor) but also economically identical to the company which has suffered the loss. The Reorganisation Tax Act indicates that economic identity will cease to exist when the organizational and business structures have changed considerably in connection with a substantial change in ownership (i.e., a transfer of at least 75% of stock ownership). Administrative guidelines stipulate in detail how the change of the organizational and business structure, as well as the change of the shareholder structure, is determined.

Shareholders

[297] If the exchange of shares falls under the Reorganisation Tax Act, the contribution may be tax neutral for the shareholders as well. The book value of the contributed shares will then form the acquisition cost of the shares received in exchange.

[298] If the exchange of shares does not fall under the Reorganisation Tax Act, the contribution is treated like the sale of shares at fair market value and the shareholders are subject to tax on the difference between the book value of their shares and the fair market value of their shares, unless the shares would qualify for an exemption such as the international participation exemption, if sold. The fair market value of the contributed shares will also form the acquisition cost for the shares received in exchange.

[299] Such share for share exchange is taxable for the shareholder in Austria only if either the shareholder is resident in Austria for tax purposes or the acquired company is resident in Austria. It does not matter where the acquiring company is resident. Double tax treaties have to be taken into account as well.

Sale and Purchase of Shares

Buyer

Direct Tax Implications

[300] When acquiring shares in another domestic company, the acquiring company must capitalize the shares at their acquisition costs. Acquisition costs also include 'incidental acquisition costs' (e.g., 'finder's fees', costs of notary public).

[301] If shares are transferred, e.g., between two sister companies, and if the transaction is not performed at arm's length, the acquiring company must capitalize the shares at an arm's length price (fair market value). The difference between an arm's length price and the actual price will be booked against the share premium account of the acquiring company (the difference is treated as a hidden contribution from the parent company to the acquiring company).

[302] In the case of a future disposal of the shares in a domestic company, by another domestic company, a capital gain is subject to corporate income tax at 25% at the level of a domestic corporation, regardless of the percentage of nominal capital held by the parent company or of the time period elapsed between acquisition and disposal of the shares. A capital gain is calculated by deducting the book value of the shares at the time of disposal from the proceeds from the sale and the costs of disposal (e.g., broker fees). The attribution of the costs of disposal to regular income or to capital gains has no practical importance, as current income and capital gains are taxed at the same rate of 25% for a corporate seller. In case of the disposal of shares in a domestic corporation by a foreign corporation, the future sale is also subject to that taxation under domestic law, but double tax treaties often allocate the taxation right to the state of residence of the seller and the state where the target is located has to exempt the sale.

[303] If the shares acquired decrease in value following the acquisition, a special write-off to the lower going concern value (*Teilwert*) of the shares may be reported on the books of the acquiring company. Generally, such special write-offs are deductible for tax purposes. However, there are some important restrictions. Due to the fact that dividends distributed by the acquired company to the acquiring company are exempt from tax under the domestic affiliation privilege, any special write-off which is caused by such dividend distributions may not be deducted for tax purposes (*ausschüttungsbedingte Teilwertabschreibung*). The same applies to losses resulting from the disposal of shares (*ausschüttungsbedingter Veräußerungsverlust*). Other special write-offs which are not caused by a reduced going concern value due to a dividend distribution of the subsidiary must be spread over a period of seven years (the same applies for losses resulting from the disposal of shares).

[304] The possibility of a depreciation of a goodwill for shares in case of the establishment of a tax group has been abolished.

Financing the Acquisition

[305] Generally, interest expenses resulting from a loan taken out to finance the acquisition of business assets are deductible at the level of the purchaser, such as an Austrian acquisition vehicle.

[306] Interest incurred in connection with the acquisition of a national or international participation may be fully deducted under certain conditions, even though the participation and the income derived from it is tax exempt. Financing costs for the financing of a tax-exempt acquisition other than interest (e.g., bank charges) are not tax deductible. The deductibility of interest is not restricted to operating corporations, therefore, deductibility is also granted to a non-operating holding company. Two exceptions apply, where interest may nevertheless not be deducted:

(1) in the case of the acquisition of shares from certain related parties; and
(2) in the case that the recipient of the interest is a low-taxed corporation.

[307] Furthermore, the interest limitation rules of Article 4 of Council Directive (EU) 2016/1164 (*Anti-Tax Avoidance Directive I*) have been implemented in section 12a of the Corporate Income Tax as of 1 January 2021. Interest expenses which exceed interest revenues (excess interest) are fully deductible up to the amount of EUR3 m only. Excess interest of more than EUR3 m is deductible only to the extent of 30% of the EBITDA.

[308] On the basis of the substance over form principle, a loan granted by a shareholder can be re-characterized into equity. Interest paid on such loans is not deductible. Even though there are no formal thin capitalization rules, the maximum debt-to-equity ratio accepted is usually around 1:4 (20% equity: 80% debt).

[309] Even if the capital provided by the shareholder qualifies as debt, the deductibility is restricted by transfer pricing considerations. Interest paid to a shareholder is deductible only to the extent that it meets the arm's length principle.

Indirect Tax Implications

[310] The transfer of shares is exempt from VAT in Austria.

Acquired Company

[311] In general, the acquisition of its shares does not change the tax position of the target company. The company is still the same legal entity and, therefore, may carry forward all its prior tax losses and other tax attributes (stand-alone approach). The purchaser generally may not benefit from the tax benefits of the acquired company (stand-alone approach). For the possibilities arising in connection with group taxation, *see* 5.2.

[312] For the restriction on the carry forward of tax losses in the case of the acquisition of a shell company, *see* paragraph [296].

Seller

[313] Capital gains arising from the disposal of shares in a domestic company are subject to corporate income tax at the regular rate of 25% for an Austrian corporate seller. Losses suffered from the disposal of shares are, in general, deductible for tax purposes. Restrictions apply if losses are caused by foregoing dividend distributions. Other losses, not related to dividend distributions, may be deducted only proportionally over a period of seven years. The restrictions, however, apply only if the shares are characterized as fixed assets; they do not apply where shares held as current assets are sold. In case of foreign corporations as sellers, the double tax treaty often allocates the taxation right to the residence state of the seller, whereas the source state has to exempt the sale.

[314] If an individual shareholder sells shares held as private assets, capital gains are taxable regardless of a minimum holding requirement and regardless of a minimum holding period. The capital gains are subject to income tax at a flat rate of 27.5%. In case of foreign individuals as sellers, the double tax treaty often allocates the taxation right to the residence state of the seller, whereas the source state has to exempt the sale.

5.4.2 Transfer of Other Assets

Contribution of Assets

[315] As mentioned before, Article III of the Reorganisation Tax Act deals with the transfer of specified assets and provides for tax exemptions at the level of the transferor and the receiving company, as well as at the level of the shareholders. The Reorganisation Tax Act is applicable only to transfers of specific assets such as a business or business unit.

[316] As a general rule, the contribution of qualifying assets is covered by the Reorganisation Tax Act if the transferor obtains shares in the receiving company as consideration. However, there are some exceptions where it is not necessary for the receiving company to issue shares. The most important case is the transfer of assets to wholly owned subsidiaries or indirect subsidiaries.

[317] If the contribution does not fall under the scope of the Reorganisation Tax Act, the transferor will be taxed on the difference between the fair market value and the book value of the assets transferred. At the level of the receiving entity, the contribution is still tax neutral, as contributions do not increase the taxable income of a company.

[318] The tax effective date (*Einbringungsstichtag*) of the transfer of assets is the date on which the assets are transferred with tax effect to the receiving company. For tax and financial purposes, the effective date may also be stipulated to be a date prior to the signing of the asset transfer contract, provided that a transfer of assets

is applied for an entry in the commercial register (in the case of the formation of a company on the basis of non-cash contributions or in the case of an increase in nominal share capital) or in all other cases reported to the tax authorities within the nine months (retroactive transfer of assets) following the effective date. Contractual relationships between the transferor and the receiving company, such as employment contracts, loans and leases of transferred assets, may typically commence only after the closing of the asset transfer contract (not the effective date).

Receiving Company

Direct Tax Implications

[319] The book values of the transferred assets, which are relevant for tax purposes at the level of the transferor, must be carried over and continued by the receiving company. For income tax purposes, the receiving company is deemed to be the legal successor of the transferor from the effective date of the transfer of assets. Shares transferred by an individual to a company must be capitalized at historical acquisition costs (maximum of their fair market value) on the balance sheet of the receiving company.

[320] If the Austrian taxation right concerning the received assets comes into existence, in general, the assets must be capitalized at their fair market value (step-up for tax purposes).

[321] Special provisions exist for cases where a participation that is subject to the international participation exemption (*see* 5.2.1 above) arises or is expanded in the course of the transfer of assets.

[322] Furthermore, any capital gains or losses resulting from the transfer of assets in the receiving company will be disregarded for tax purposes, unless they result from the fusion of assets and liabilities (confusio).

[323] Loss carry-forwards of the transferor may be utilized in the future by the receiving company to the extent that they are attributable to the transferred assets, provided that the latter exist at the effective date of the transfer. For the restriction on the carry forward of tax losses in the case of the acquisition of a shell company, *see* 5.4.1.

[324] If the transferor receives shares of the receiving company in consideration of the transferred assets, the shares must be capitalized at the net book value of the transferred assets. Special rules apply where assets are transferred into a subsidiary, a sister company or a parent company.

Indirect Tax Implications

[325] Transfers of assets carried out under the rules set out in the Reorganisation Tax Act are not subject to VAT.

[326] Furthermore, transfers of assets are exempt from stamp duties if the transferred assets have belonged to the transferor for at least two years at the date of the conclusion of the asset transfer contract. For details concerning the real estate transfer tax, *see* 5.2.4.

Transferring Company

[327] Generally, the transferor is not deemed to realize a taxable gain on the assets transferred to the receiving company if Austria retains its taxation right. If Austria loses its taxation right or the taxation right of Austria is restricted after the transfer, the transfer is taxable (exit taxation). In the case of a transfer to EU or EEA countries (only for EEA countries with broad administrative and enforcement assistance), the exit taxation regime provides for an option to apply for the payment of exit tax in instalments over a period of:

- five years for exit tax for capital gains of fixed assets; and
- two years for exit tax for capital gains of current assets.

[328] If exit taxation does not apply, the assets are transferred at book values (*Buchwertfortführung*) from the perspective of the transferor. If a trade or business, a separate division of a trade or business, a partnership interest or a qualifying shareholding held as business property is transferred, a transfer balance sheet must be prepared on which the transferred assets are reported at their book values as at the effective date of the transfer of assets.

[329] The Reorganisation Tax Act contains special valuation rules for cross-border transfers of assets.

[330] Furthermore, subsequent to section 16 paragraph 5 of the Reorganisation Tax Act, the scope of the transferred assets may be extended or restricted retroactively as per the effective date of the contribution in specific cases, for example, by adding an additional liability of the receiving entity against the transferor.

[331] This liability allows a reduction of the value of the transferred assets by allocating an additional account payable by the receiving company to the transferor. This additional account payable may not exceed 50% of the fair market value of the transferred assets.

[332] If the tax book value of the transferred assets becomes negative as a result of cash withdrawals or allocation of additional liabilities under section 16 paragraph 5 of the Reorganisation Tax Act, the negative amount is classified as a dividend to the contributing party. Cash withdrawals are deemed to be distributed one week after the notification of the contribution. The allocation of additional liabilities under section 16 paragraph 5 of the Reorganisation Tax Act is generally deemed to be paid at the settlement of the liability.

Sale and Purchase of Assets

Buyer

Direct Tax Implications

[333] Generally, the acquired assets must be reported at their acquisition costs on the books of the acquiring company. This principle applies in the case of an acquisition of separate assets, as well as an acquisition of an entire business.

[334] The difference between the price actually paid for a business or separate division of a business and the acquisition costs of the individual assets must be reported as goodwill. If a single price is paid for a business, the price must be attributed to the transferred assets according to the going concern values of the individual assets of the business in order to determine the acquisition costs of the assets (i.e., step-up for depreciation purposes). The remaining acquisition costs that are not allocable to the transferred assets must be reported as goodwill. Where specific prices are indicated in the contract for each asset, the tax authorities may seek to amend the acquisition costs of the assets if the agreed prices are found not to be at arm's length. This may be the case if the parties attempt to shift most of the price of a business to assets depreciable over a short period of time, or if the price for individual assets is reported as relatively low for real estate transfer tax purposes. For the treatment of goodwill, *see* 5.5 below.

[335] The acquiring company is not entitled to utilize any tax losses available to the selling company in respect of the transferred business. Tax benefits of the seller may generally not be transferred to the purchaser.

[336] Costs other than financing costs which accrue in connection with the acquisition of a business may be so-called additional acquisition costs (*Anschaffungsnebenkosten*). Such additional acquisition costs must be capitalized and added to the acquisition cost on the purchaser's balance sheet. They may consequently be depreciated.

Indirect Tax Implications

[337] The disposal of assets, even a whole business, is subject to VAT in Austria. Austria has not opted for a tax exemption for a transfer of a business according to Article 19 of Council Directive 2006/112/EC (VAT Directive).

[338] The sale of a business as a going concern is therefore treated like the sale of the underlying individual assets in Austria. Therefore, the purchase price must be allocated to the individual assets. Tax rates and exemptions are applicable under regular VAT law. The goodwill is subject to 20% VAT.

[339] However, the buyer may obtain a credit of the input VAT if he is a taxable person and he is acquiring the assets for his business.

[340] The assignment of accounts receivable is subject to a stamp duty at a rate of 0.8% under the Stamp Duty Act (*Gebührengesetz*; *GebG*) (*see* also 5.2.6 above). The tax base is the consideration for the assignment. The same applies to a transfer of other rights. The assignment of receivables in the course of a transfer of a going concern, however, may be structured in a way that it is exempt from the stamp duty.

[341] For details concerning the real estate tax, *see* 5.2.4 above.

Seller

[342] Any capital gain resulting from the disposal of assets or of a business or a separate division of a business is subject to corporate income tax at the standard rate of 25% if the seller is a corporation. In principle, there is no difference between the taxation of capital gains resulting from the disposal of a business and capital gains resulting from the disposal of other assets.

[343] Capital losses resulting from the disposal of assets or of businesses or separate divisions of businesses may be deducted for tax purposes and treated in the same way as losses resulting from current activities, without restriction. In case of a corporation, the offsetting of losses suffered in previous years (loss carryforwards) is, however, restricted to 75% of the profits of the respective year, so that at least 25% of the taxable profit remains within the charge to tax, unless a business or a business unit is sold by this corporation. In case of a sale of single assets by a corporation, the 75% restriction regarding the deduction of losses from previous years usually applies.

[344] If the seller is an individual, the taxation of capital gains resulting from the disposal of assets of a business is taxed at the personal income tax rate of up to 55%. However, if an individual sells a business or a separate division of a business, special provisions apply. In general, the taxpayer may choose between the following alternatives:

- taxation of the total amount of the capital gain in the current year with a tax exemption of EUR7 300 in the case of the disposal of a business (or a proportional amount in the case of the disposal of a separate division of a business);
- the capital gain may be allocated to and taxed over three years if the taxpayer has operated his business for at least seven years; or
- for taxpayers who have died, are permanently unable to work or are aged 60 or more and are retiring, the rate is reduced to half of the average tax rate if the taxpayer has operated his business for at least seven years.

5.4.3 Withholding Taxes

[345] Payments to non-residents (and even payments to residents) may be subject to withholding taxes. The most important withholding taxes are:

- Dividend withholding tax for dividends paid by Austrian companies (27.5% in case of payments to individuals, 25% in case of payments to corporations).
- Interest withholding tax on publicly offered bonds issued by Austrian obligors, saving accounts with Austrian banks and other interest except for private loans (usually 27.5%, in some cases 25%).
- Withholding tax on capital gains of shares deposited in Austrian bank deposits (27.5%).
- Wage tax on employment income derived from Austrian employers or foreign employers with Austrian permanent establishments (at the progressive income tax rate of up to 55%).
- Withholding tax on the sale of private real estate (30%).

[346] Special withholding taxes for payments to non-residents are:

- Royalty withholding tax (20%).
- Withholding tax on payments for personnel leases from abroad (20%).
- Withholding taxes for payments for lecturers, commercial and technical consultants, artists, sportsmen, supervisory board members, income from real

estate investment funds and many more (section 99 of the Austrian Income Tax Act).

[347] Interest paid to foreign corporate/group shareholders or affiliates is not subject to withholding taxes in Austria if the underlying transaction is a private loan (not a publicly placed bond or a bank deposit).

[348] Pursuant to section 99a of the Austrian Income Tax Act, implementing the EU Interest Royalties Directive, royalties paid to related companies may be exempted from withholding tax.

[349] Similarly, dividends paid to EU resident corporate shareholders may be exempted from withholding tax according to section 94 paragraph 2 of the Austrian Income Tax Act, implementing the EU Parent-Subsidiary-Directive. For a relief at source, the foreign shareholder has to meet certain substance requirements. In a refund procedure, it has to be established that no abuse of law exists, in particular, that the EU company has been interposed merely to obtain withholding tax relief that otherwise would not have been obtained.

[350] Payments to non-residents in respect of the purchase or renting of commercial immovable property are not subject to a withholding tax.

[351] Austria has concluded double tax treaties with more than ninety countries in the world. In many cases, depending on the rules of each double tax treaty, Austria may be obliged to grant relief from its source taxation either fully or partially. In order to procure treaty relief, two different procedures are available:

(1) the source relief; and
(2) the refund procedure.

[352] To obtain a relief at source, the recipient has to provide a certificate of a residence and confirm that it meets certain substance requirements. In some cases, relief at source is not possible at all (e.g., hidden profit distributions, letterbox companies, legal entities that have their place of effective management in a country different from the country of establishment).

5.4.4 Thin Capitalization

[353] There are no statutory thin capitalization rules in Austria. However, the Supreme Administrative Court (*Verwaltungsgerichtshof*) has established certain broad guidelines, which are used to determine whether funds provided by shareholders to a company are to be treated as debt or equity.

[354] First of all, funds provided as debt to the company may be treated as such only if the company's equity can be deemed economically sufficient for the company's purposes. Whether the company's capital is economically sufficient must be determined on a case-by-case basis, taking into account the company's overall economic situation. Thus, if the company faces the imminent risk of insolvency, there is a certain risk that any capital provided to it by its shareholders will be treated as equity rather than debt, leading to the fact that any payments made in respect of the funds provided will be treated as deemed profit distributions (e.g., dividends) and not as interest payments. Such deemed profit distributions, however, do not constitute tax-deductible expenses.

[355] Second, hybrid capital instruments may be treated as either debt or equity, depending on their terms and conditions, as evaluated on a case-by-case basis. If payments connected to hybrid capital recognized as equity are made, any such payments are treated as deemed profit distributions and thus do not constitute tax-deductible expenses.

[356] Third, if the funds are treated as debt, interest payments are only fully tax deductible if the underlying contract between the company and its shareholders is at arm's length. If this is not the case, the difference between the interest paid and the amount of interest considered to be at arm's length is treated as a deemed profit distribution by the company to its shareholders, subject to the condition that the interest actually paid to be higher than the arm's length amount. If the interest paid is less than the arm's length amount, a hidden equity contribution by the shareholders to the company in the amount of the difference is assumed.

[357] Finally, no deduction is possible for interest paid to a corporation if:

- the payer and recipient are, directly or indirectly, part of the same group or under the same controlling shareholder; and
- the recipient (or the beneficial owner, if different) is (a) due to a comprehensive personal or material tax exemption not subject to corporate income tax in its state of residence; (b) subject to corporate income tax at a rate of less than 10%; or (c) due to an applicable reduction subject to an effective tax rate of less than 10%.

[358] Furthermore, the interest limitation rules of Article 4 of Council Directive (EU) 2016/1164 (*Anti-Tax Avoidance Directive I*) have been implemented in section 12a of the Corporate Income Tax as of 1 January 2021. Interest expenses which exceed interest revenues (excess interest) are fully deductible up to the amount of EUR3 m only. Excess interest of more than EUR3 m is deductible only to the extent of 30% of the EBITDA.

5.4.5 Transfer Pricing

[359] Austrian transfer pricing rules generally follow OECD standards. In 2010, the Federal Ministry of Finance issued Transfer Pricing Guidelines which broadly follow the OECD transfer pricing guidelines.

[360] In particular, if an M&A transaction is carried out between related parties and the consideration for the shares or other assets is not at arm's length, the acquisition cost of the assets will be adjusted to the arm's length price under the transfer pricing rules. Likewise, the sale price of the selling entity will be adjusted.

[361] The companies will then have a transfer pricing receivable or liability against each other. If these receivables or liabilities are not redeemed, it may constitute hidden profit distributions or hidden contributions under Austrian law.

[362] Hidden contributions are tax neutral. Hidden distributions are not deductible and may result in withholding tax liabilities (25% for hidden distributions to foreign corporations).

5.5 Treatment of Goodwill

5.5.1 Assets

[363] For tax purposes, the goodwill must be depreciated over a period of fifteen years on a straight-line basis. The period may be shorter in specific cases.

5.5.2 Shares

[364] The depreciation of a goodwill for shares was abolished in 2014. Only for acquisitions before 1 March 2014 it is possible to continue the depreciation of a goodwill over fifteen years.

6 EMPLOYMENT CONSIDERATIONS

6.1 Legislative Framework

[365] Labour and employment are regulated by a great number of federal statutes. Therefore, Austrian labour law is a field composed of a large variety of sources on different levels. Additionally, more detailed terms of regulation and conditions of employment are provided by collective bargaining agreements (*Kollektivvertrag*). These contracts are concluded between employers' and employees' organizations, each responsible for a specific group of businesses. They are binding on the individual employer and employee of the relevant group irrespective of whether or not they have explicitly been made part of the employment contract. Collective bargaining agreements typically contain rules regarding minimum salaries or wages, special payments like holiday and Christmas bonuses or working hours.

[366] In Austria, statutory law and collective agreements reserve several matters to be dealt with by so-called shop agreements (*Betriebsvereinbarung*) which are written contracts concluded between an employer and the works council. Within such limits, a shop agreement has the legal force of a statute, granting individual rights to employees which can only be changed in favour of the employee by individual contract.

6.2 Employment Protection

6.2.1 Representation

Supervisory Board/Co-determination

[367] The Austrian Stock Corporation Act provides for a two-tier board structure composed of the management board and the supervisory board. In some instances, this structure also applies to limited liability companies. The management board is responsible for the day-to-day business, while the supervisory board mainly monitors these activities and particularly resolves statutory and assigned matters. If a works council is established, the Austrian Labour Constitution Act (*Arbeitsverfassungsgesetz*; *ArbVG*) entitles employees to delegate representatives to the supervisory board in accordance with the principles of one-third parity (*Drittelparität*). One-third of the supervisory board's members are delegated by the employees, the other two-thirds of its members are elected by the shareholders. Thus, employee representatives may gain insights and are entitled to the same level of information as shareholder delegates and, most notably, may actively take part in important business decisions.

Obligations of Information or Consultation Relating to M&A Transactions

Information Rights of Employees

[368] Potential information rights of employees depend on whether a share deal or an asset deal took place. Only with regard to assets deals and provided that there is no works council in an undertaking or establishment, the seller or the buyer must inform the employees affected by the transfer of the undertaking or establishment in advance in writing of the date or the planned date of the transfer, the reason for the transfer, the legal, economic and social consequences of the transfer for the employees and the measures envisaged to mitigate these consequences. The employees cannot prevent such a transaction but may object to the transfer of their employment relationships in certain limited circumstances (*see* 6.2.2). When a works council is established, the duty to provide information is only given towards the works council.

Rights of Works Councils

[369] Under the provisions of the Labour Constitution Act, the proprietor of a business unit (*Betriebsinhaber*) is obliged to inform the works council in advance of planned changes in operations in order to enable the works council to assess in detail the possible effects of the planned measure and to give an opinion on such measure. At the request of the works council, the employer must consult with the works council on the respective measure. The following measures, in particular, are considered to be such changes in operations:

- cutback or closure of a business or part of a business;
- mass layoff;
- transfer of a business or part of a business to another location;

- merger with another business;
- change in the scope of a business, the facilities, work and business organization, or the organization of branches within a business;
- introduction of new working methods;
- introduction of substantial restructuring and automation processes;
- change of the legal form or the ownership of a business.

[370] In case of a share deal, in legal literature, some authors argue that since the employer remains the same, there is no such obligation to inform the works council. However, especially in case all or a majority of shares are sold, it is argued that the works council must be informed about this 'important change' in ownership. With regard to an asset deal, the works council must be informed about the date of and reason for the transfer as well as its legal, economic and social consequences and measures taken to mitigate these consequences.

[371] The works council cannot prevent the transaction but can only propose different approaches. In addition, if an envisaged change results in a significant disadvantage for a major part of the employees (e.g., mass layoffs), the works council can enforce the conclusion of a social plan setting forth additional employee entitlements provided that at least twenty employees are permanently employed in the operation.

6.2.2 Principle of Continuity

[372] The Employment Contract Law Adaption Act (*Arbeitsvertragsrechts-Anpassungsgesetz*; *AVRAG*) provides that the acquisition of a business unit (e.g., by way of an asset deal) leads to a mandatory automatic transfer of all employment contracts that are part of the affected business unit. Therefore, it is not possible to 'pick and choose' employees, but the acquirer rather assumes the employment contracts as they exist at the time of the transfer, including all benefits, unsettled claims, unconsumed vacation and severance pay entitlements. Employees may object to the transfer of their employment relationships only in certain limited circumstances, e.g., if any provisions on protection against termination as provided by a collective bargaining agreement or any pension commitments of the selling side are not taken over. Furthermore, employees are granted an extraordinary right to terminate their contract if working conditions worsen significantly. By contrast, terminations by the employer due to the acquisition of the business unit or transfer of the labour relations are null and void if no objective reasons requiring termination can be proven.

6.2.3 Termination of Employment

[373] Generally speaking, an employment contract may be terminated either by mutual agreement, by giving notice or by dismissal.

[374] The relevant labour laws set out minimum notice periods to be given by each party, the length of which depends on how long the employee has been employed in the company. The employer and the employee each have the right to terminate the employment contract with immediate effect for important reasons. The labour laws give a list of causes in which an immediate termination is possible.

[375] Furthermore, the relevant labour laws grant special status to certain groups of employees, such as pregnant or disabled persons, apprentices, and members of the works council. These groups enjoy increased protection regarding the termination of their contracts. Older employees also benefit from a certain degree of protection against dismissal, particularly when such dismissal would result in social hardship or would otherwise substantially violate their justified interests (e.g., difficulties in finding a new job due to older age or age discrimination). Next to that, some employees could be entitled to the old severance payment scheme which grants such employees a multiple of their monthly salary depending on, and increasing with, their term of service.

[376] Taking all of the aforementioned into account, intended (post-closing) restructuring measures may become more difficult and/or costly to implement.

[377] In case of a mass layoff, the employer has to notify the Labour Market Service (*Arbeitsmarktservice*; *AMS*).

6.2.4 Trade Unions

[378] Even though the number is declining, still 35% of all Austrian employees are represented by the Austrian Trade Union Federation (*Österreichischer Gewerkschaftsbund*; *ÖGB*), which makes it a highly influential and powerful voluntary association. Traditionally, there are almost no strikes or lockouts in Austria. 'Compromise' is the keyword in Austria's industrial relations.

[379] This unique working relationship has become known worldwide under the informal label of the 'Social Partnership' (*Sozialpartnerschaft*). For the past fifty years, this effective means of cooperation between employers and employees has been successfully practised in Austria.

6.3 Pensions

6.3.1 Statutory Pension Insurance

[380] Austria has a statutory pension system, established under the Social Insurance Act (*Allgemeines Sozialversicherungsgesetz*; *ASVG*). This system is funded by employer and employee contributions to social security.

[381] Generally, the following benefits are covered by mandatory pension insurance:

- old-age pensions;
- pensions to widows and widowers or orphans; and
- disability pensions.

[382] For women, the pension age is currently 60, and for men, the age is 65. The retirement age for women will be gradually aligned with that of men from 2024 until 2033. The pension is paid by the social security authorities. However, there are options to retire earlier or at a later stage (e.g., early retirement, corridor pension).

6.3.2 Company Pension Plans

[383] Under Austrian law, employers have no obligation to grant additional company pension schemes or to establish employee pension plans. However, employees may be entitled to a company pension (in addition to the above-mentioned statutory pension), if the employer concludes individual agreements or shop agreements on company pensions.

[384] The legal basis for private pension agreements is the Company Pension Act (*Betriebspensionsgesetz*; *BPG*), which essentially covers the following three indifferent types of pensions:

(1) defined benefit systems;
(2) defined contribution systems (usually using a pension fund); and
(3) life insurances.

6.3.3 M&A Transactions

[385] In case of an M&A transaction, the buyer can refuse to take over company pension commitments based on individual contracts if the transfer of business does not take place by way of universal succession. In this case, the employee can either object to the transfer of the employment relationship or ask for a compensatory lump-sum payment to be made by the seller.

[386] If, however, a company pension plan is based on a collective bargaining agreement or shop agreement, the buyer cannot refuse to continue the plan. A shop agreement, however, could be terminated which basically leads to a situation comparable to the existence of contractual commitments as mentioned above.

6.4 Retention of Key Management and Employees

[387] In case of an asset deal, all employees working for the transferred business unit will also be transferred to the buyer. No further steps shall be taken by the seller to ensure retention. However, Members of the executive board (Vorstandsmitglieder) of a public limited company (AG) are not covered by the legal framework. Managing directors of a limited liability company (GmbH) with more than 50% of the shares are not covered by the legal framework; managing directors with more than 25% are not covered, provided they have a 'blocking minority'. It is, therefore, necessary to either conclude new employment contracts with them or to agree on a tripartite transfer of the employment contract.

[388] In case of a share deal, the employer will remain the same and no further steps must be taken.

[389] Post-contractual non-compete and non-solicitation clauses can be agreed upon in the employment contracts. Non-compete clauses, as well as non-solicitation clauses referring to customers, can only be agreed on for a period of one year after termination. Such clauses will not be enforceable in case the employer gives notice, terminates immediately without cause, gives cause for immediate termination by the employee or if the salary of the employee is not high enough upon termination (in 2022: EUR3 780). Non-solicitation clauses concerning other employees can be agreed for up to three years.

6.5 Treatment of Foreign Employees

6.5.1 Residence Permit (*Aufenthaltsbewilligung*)

[390] Under Austrian law (*Ausländerbeschäftigungsgesetz*; *AuslBG*), the following persons do not need to apply for a work permit:

- EU/EEA citizens and Swiss citizens.
- Third-country nationals who are family members (spouse and minors) of Austrian citizens.
- Spouses and minors of EEA citizens and Swiss citizens.
- Parents and parents-in-law of EEA citizens.
- Asylum-seeker with asylum decision.

[391] In general, the employment of Non-EU/EEA nationals requires a residence permit and a work permit. Some of the permits available cover both residency and access to the labour market. There are different kinds of permits issued by the Immigration Office. The most common ones are:

- Red-White-Red Card (*Rot-Weiß-Rot-Karte*) which is valid for two years but requires an achievement of minimum points based on education, age, prior years of service, prior salaries, language skills, etc.
- Red-White-Red Card plus (*Rot-Weiß-Rot-Karte Plus*) which can only be obtained as an extension of a normal Red-White-Red Card or Blue Card-EU.
- Blue Card-EU (*Blaue Karte-EU*) is applicable for skilled foreign employees holding an undergraduate degree with guaranteed minimum wage of 1.5 times the Austrian average gross annual salary. Permanent Residency EU (*Daueraufenthalt-EU*) which may be granted after uninterrupted establishment for five years and it is equivalent to unlimited residence entitlement.

6.5.2 Work Permit (*Beschäftigungsbewilligung*)

[392] A work permit has to be applied for by the employer at the competent Labour Market Service unless it is one of the permits also covering residency. In such case, residency authorities are competent to decide (e.g., MA35 in Vienna).

[393] Work permits entitle the employer to employ an individual person for a particular position. A work permit may be issued for a maximum period of one year and the working relationship must be started six weeks after authorization; otherwise, the work permit expires.

[394] The Labour Market Service may issue a work permit only under certain circumstances. In general, it has to be determined whether the current state and development of the labour market allows the employment of foreigners. Other important public or economic reasons have to be taken into account as well before a work permit may be granted. Further criteria are listed in the relevant laws.

[395] Special provisions apply to Turkish citizens and Ukrainian refugees. Due to an association agreement between Austria and Turkey, Turkish citizens obtain better access to the labour market. For Ukrainian refugees, access to the labour market is also possible through a simplified procedure.

[396] Under Austrian law, it is an offence to employ a foreign person without valid permission. In case of violation, the competent authorities may levy fines against the employer. Should the violation be repeated, the fines may be doubled, and it can also be decided that the employer is no longer allowed to employ foreigners.

www.ingramcontent.com/pod-product-compliance
Lightning Source LLC
Chambersburg PA
CBHW071358230926
51846CB00002B/592
9789403523965